SCHOONER CAPTAIN

Schooner Captain

THE STORY OF CAPTAIN HUGH SHAW
FOR HALF A CENTURY
A MASTER IN SAIL IN BRITISH WATERS

compiled and edited by
NORAH AYLAND

D. BRADFORD BARTON LTD
TRURO

copyright © 1972   Norah Ayland

published by
D. BRADFORD BARTON LTD
TRETHELLAN HOUSE
TRURO

printed by H. E. Warne Ltd   St. Austell

CONTENTS

CHAPTER I *My childhood days – St. Mark's school – Connah's Quay – to become a captain – a Liverpool 'flat' – my first experience of the sea – Old Jimmy – the tug boats – Dee-side* 9

CHAPTER II *The schooner* Alfred *– the great gale of November 1890 – a trip to Pentewan – the* Earl of Lathom *– the* Enterprise *– the* Tide Watch 15

CHAPTER III *We move to Flint in 1895 – soup kitchens – at sea on the* Mary Elizabeth *– Limerick – Innishmore – the local magistrate – Mullaghmore – the missing hour – Scotland – 'Go scrape the mast' – in court – the captain's hoard of food* 21

CHAPTER IV *The* Emma *and* Esther *– the* Not Forgot *– cargoes for Ireland – the* Lizzie *– from Gravesend with a cargo of explosives – ordinary seaman on the* Sunbeam *– the* Elizabeth Hyam *– the* Hilda *– I join the* Victor *as mate – the* Isabella 33

CHAPTER V *Well here I was, Captain – the* Elizabeth Hyam *– my Uncle Tom as Mate – the Races – Menai Straits – the frightened mate – the lost anchor at Barrow – a cargo for Cemlyn Bay* 45

CHAPTER VI *My schooner* J.C.R. *– I become captain of the* Sarah Latham *– loss of the* J.C.R. *– the* Lady Fielding *at Abersoch – a collision with the trawler* Lucerne *– the irate owner* 57

CHAPTER VII *Discharging cargoes – have you paid your 'income tax'? – voyages to the Solway Firth – to Preston off the Bar Buoy – Arlingham on Severn – a meeting* 69

CHAPTER VIII *Part owner of the* Kate of Barrow, *1911 – windbound at Holyhead – a gale at Christmastime – loss of the* Harvest Queen *– a cargo to Cardigan* 76

Chapter IX   The outbreak of World War I – my father joins as Mate – cargoes to Ireland – Youghal – Clonakilty – coal to France – a dangerous trade – the Kindly Light – the Katie Cluett – the little pilot – the Armistice   79

Chapter X   Trading to France with coal and pit props – profitable charters – the Mary Miller – at Portmadoc – an engine for Kate   93

Chapter XI   Ireland and the Troubles – Moorhill Quay – Youghal Light – I purchase the ketch Irene – also the schooner Camborne – Limerick – Valentia Island – a lull in the fighting   97

Chapter XII   Trading round Ireland – Killorglin – 'This vessel sunk by rebels' – bacon for Liverpool – engine trouble on the Camborne   108

Chapter XIII   On board the Camborne – Paulo, the dog – a storm at Arthurstown – a gale in 1927 – the loss of the Excel – in Gloucester   121

Chapter XIV   Hard times – the Irene and Kate are sold – a cargo from the wreck Nordstad – my sons aboard on holiday – trouble at Kilmakilloge – a voyage light from Tralee – buying Irish scrap iron   127

Chapter XV   John Kennedy – becalmed off Land's End – on the rocks off Jersey – repairs at Par – a tragedy in the Bristol Channel – back to Ireland – salt and scrap iron   133

Chapter XVI   The Camborne – our experiences in the terrible gale of February 1936 – back to Tralee – Fenit and a new propeller – Youghal   139

Chapter XVII   War again – our Irish trading continues – mines and a fire at sea – the schooner Ryelands – 1946, my two schooners Camborne and Ryelands sold – the motor coaster Eldorita – I bring my story to an end   145

ILLUSTRATIONS

Captain Hugh Shaw	65
His father, Captain Humphrey Shaw	65
Connah's Quay in the 1880's	66
The Quay House at Connah's Quay	66
The two-masted schooner Kindly Light	83
Captain Shaw's schooner Camborne	83
Three views on board the Camborne	84
Coasting schooners in Penarth Roads, 1930	101
The ketch Irene, bought by Captain Shaw in 1922	102
Windbound in Menai Straits, about 1900	102
The schooner Ryelands, owned for a time by Captain Shaw	119
The Elizabeth Hyam, Captain Shaw's first command	120
Eldorita, entering Penzance harbour in the 1950's	120

CHAPTER I

Childhood days – St. Mark's school – Connah's Quay – to become a captain – a Liverpool 'flat' – my first experience of the sea – Old Jimmy – the tug boats – Dee-side

I WAS BORN ON THE 15TH DAY OF OCTOBER 1881, IN THE house next door to the Halfway House Inn at Connah's Quay, on the Dee near Chester. I do not remember much that happened here in those early days of my childhood, apart from being close to the railway line and feeling frightened when the trains rushed past, and seeing vessels passing by on the River Dee which flowed close to where we lived. I have very early memories of living in a thatched cottage in the country, for my parents had moved there from Connah's Quay. The cottage was close to a large house known as the Vron Hall, it was situated at the foot of a steep hill and The Hall was at the top. There, I remember, standing by the cottage door, listening to the faint strains of a band playing in the streets of Connah's Quay, some two miles away. At times, the music would be quite clear, then, the wind would carry the sound away and I would only hear the beat of the drum. I believe that was the first sound of music I had ever heard and it was a great delight to me.

My father was a coasting sea captain, and among my earliest recollections are memories of the happy days when he came home from sea. These were days of great excitement and pleasure to us all. I think it was then that I made up my mind to be a sailor when I grew up and I also hoped there would be someone who would be as excited and happy to see me as I was to welcome my father home again. On looking back I now realise that our family fortunes had not been good when we were living in the cottage, but as soon as my father's prospects improved we moved back again to Connah's Quay.

I started school at St. Mark's and everything seemed very strange to me after the lonely surroundings of the cottage, and the children there did not appear to take kindly to me at first. When I grew older, like all the boys of my age who lived at the 'Quay', I thought of no calling other than the sea, and with this in mind, our wise schoolmaster, Mr. Woodcock, constantly emphasised to us the necessity of hard work and the importance of mathematics. He was very strict if the boys failed to take an interest in their lessons and consequently many of his pupils obtained their foreign master's certificate and took command of ocean liners.

In those days, the only industry at the 'Quay' was that which was connected with the sea, and most boys on leaving school became either a sailor, a shipwright, a sailmaker or an assistant in a shop supplying the vessels that sailed in and out of this little port. Some went to work in the docks, but as a rule, the dockers were sailors who had grown tired of the hard life at sea, and had returned to work on the 'acre' as the space which comprised the dock area was called. The successful men of the port were those who commanded the finest schooners, and some were able to make a good living and to retire at quite an early age but there were many who were unsuccessful and these would go from ship to ship; trying to better themselves, often taking a mate's berth or anything that offered, if times were difficult.

To become a coasting sea captain and to be given command of a ketch or a schooner, the procedure was that a young seaman, with some years of experience as able seaman and mate in these craft, and having sufficient confidence in himself that he could take command of a ship on the coastal trade, would apply for a berth as master, or seek out an owner in need of a captain. Prospective captains were usually the sons of seafaring families or the sons of shipowners. Having secured the promise of a berth, he would next have to pass a seamanship test. Seamanship tests were conducted by, in this area, The Naval Mutual Insurance Society, known as The Dee Club. The Society also insured the vessels. The test was an examination of the applicant, as to his abilities and his qualifications, carried out by the Secretary and the Manager of the 'Club', together with the assistance of a couple of retired captains of long experience. Their method was to spread a chart on a table, on which they placed the model of a ship, and the prospective captain was told to work the ship from one supposed port to another. Questions were asked as to the direction and force of the wind and the state of the tides, and as to how he would extricate his ship from all manner of dangerous and desperate situations. If he satisfied his examiners he would then be in a position to take command and he would indeed be very fortunate if he started in a fine new ship, for in most cases the only berths available would be in a poor old vessel, in which it would be almost impossible to make a living, and whatever his fortune, it would depend on how well the vessel paid the owner as to whether or not he would be offered a better and larger ship.

The vessels were sailed on a 'Thirds' share system, e.g. if the freight came to £60, the master took for his share two thirds of it, (i.e. £40) out of which he paid his crew a monthly wage, fed them and paid all port charges. The owner from his share of the freight, maintained the ship.

My father was one of the unsuccessful captains, which was not hard to understand when I think of the dreadful craft in which he had to prove his ability to succeed. These vessels were old, were round bowed and required a lot of ballast. They were also deep draughted and were described as slow old coffins. The boys at school knew the history and status of all the craft out of this port and I was conscious at school that they were well aware of my father's lack of status in the schooner line. Nevertheless, even at that early age I used to think that no one was superior to my father, because to me he was the best man in the world. He had many ups and downs when we were young, and during a bad spell when he was out of a berth, he took charge of a wretched old craft known as a 'Liverpool Flat'. She had no bulwarks and only one mast, and she traded solely in the river, carrying coal from the Point of Ayr Colliery to the Chemical Works in Flint.

I was eight years old when I went for my first trip with my father in this craft. I think he must have taken me for company for she was a one man ship. We went to the Point of Ayr to join her and as there was a period of stormy weather, we remained in the shelter of the port for two days. On the third day the wind died away and we towed out to the deep water and sailed to the anchorage in Mostyn Deeps, or Wildroads as it was usually called, where we anchored to await the tug to tow us on the next tide to Flint. As night came on, the wind began to freshen, and soon after midnight it was blowing a full gale from the north-west, causing a big sea to get up and the old 'Flat' to drag her anchor.

At last, she grounded, striking the sandbank heavily and she pounded for hours with the waves breaking over her. My father and I were wet and cold and we were in darkness, for sea water had got into the cabin and had extinguished our lamp. The misery of that night would remain with me always.

We had grounded on a sandbank near Mostyn and when daylight came, my father said to me, 'Hugh, you must get away from here and go home.'

Now all vessels were compelled to have a small boat and ours was secured to our stern. My father made a long rope fast to the boat and told me to get into it, saying as I did so that he would slack away until she touched the hard bottom, when he would expect me to jump into the shallow water and wade ashore. I did as he told me and waded to dry land. It did not matter about getting wet for we had been wet for hours. When I reached the shore I turned to watch my father pull the small boat back to the 'Flat' and then I waved to him and set off for the embankment that runs from Mostyn to Llannerch-y-mor, where I could reach the main road. I scrambled up the embankment and there I felt the full force of the wind, blowing right in my back, hurrying me along, and at times almost taking me off my feet. Even now I fancy I can still feel that wind.

It was some ten miles from here to my home in Connah's Quay. Reaching the main road I found it quite deserted, and between walking and being blown along I came at last to the little port of Bagillt. I had an aunt who lived here and I decided that I would go to her home. When she saw the condition I was in, she became very distressed and she quickly took me in and removed my wet clothes. Wrapping me in a blanket, she seated me near the fire, gave me a good meal and set about drying my clothes. As soon as I was dressed and ready to leave, my aunt took me to the station where she put me on a train bound for home, having first paid my fare. It is good to look back on kindness such as this. I arrived home, none the worse for my adventure and I remember nothing more until next day, when, at midday on my way back to school, I met my father walking home. It appears, the old 'Flat' had been towed off the bank and had been taken to her discharging berth in Flint. My father, having finished with the vessel, had been to see the owner to settle accounts. The owner, who also owned an hotel and lived in it, after listening to my father's story of the hardships of the trip, gave him some whisky. By the time I met him, the whisky had gone to his head. I, of course, was very pleased to see him, especially so after leaving him in such a wretched state. He stopped when he saw me and stood as stiff as a ramrod. He looked very serious indeed.

I smiled at him and said, 'Hello Dad.'

He looked at me for some time without speaking, then, realising he was too light headed to talk sensibly, muttered, 'Hugh, it is no use talking to me, I am slightly intoxicated.' He walked past me. I watched him for a few minutes and then went on my way to school.

In school, we took our lessons to the sound of the caulking irons being struck by the carpenters' mallets and to the scream of the steam saw as it cut through the hard oak used for building vessels. This oak would lie along the roadside leading to the shipyard, where it would dry and season for months before it was ready for use. At this time, fine ships were being built in the yard by the firm of Messrs. Fergusson and Baird, and one of the partners, Mr. James Baird, lived in a house in the shipyard area.

We boys knew all that was going on in the yard and were often chased out by 'Old Jimmy' (our name for Mr. Baird). We were very wary of him for he would not allow boys to play around, mostly because of the risks involved in climbing in dangerous places.

We boys often went to the docks, where small brigs and other craft were arriving, laden with timber from the Baltic ports. Many were foreign vessels and some of them were so old and unseaworthy that they never loaded another cargo, remaining here to be eventually broken up. It was an exciting sight to see a large schooner arrive behind the tug. The tide runs very fast here and there is not much room to swing the vessel head to tide than the vessel's length. When the tug's engine stopped turning the propeller, the tow rope became slack and it would then be made fast with a slip rope to the tug's stern; so that, when the rope took the strain, with the vessel's way it would swing the tug's bow, head on to the tide. The schooner keeping close to the quay side. When the tug's head pointed downstream, the vessel being towed, would put the helm hard-a-port and with the tow ropes taking the strain, she would come head to tide swinging in her own length. With these manoeuvres we often expected damage would be done, but that happened very rarely.

There were three fine tug boats in the port. Two were owned by the firm of shipowners and shipbrokers, now known as Coppack Bros, then known as Coppack and Carter. One was called the *Taliesin* and we boys thought it was the most powerful tug boat in the world. The second was called the *Albert* and the third the *Manxman*, owned by the Great Western Railway and she was used for towing vessels to their wharf at Saltney.

Messrs Coppack had a ship's chandlery store in Dock Road and above the shop was their shipbrokering office. A well known feature of this building was a space on the ground floor which was a meeting place for captains, who, when home would congregate and while away the hours spinning yarns.

The pilots for all the ports on the Dee estuary lived in Connah's Quay and they used to take it in turn to cruise outside the estuary, to pilot ships bound for any port from Rhyl to Chester. Most of these little ports are now silted up and forgotten. Such a one was the little port of Bagillt. I remember a small steamer called the *Alice Capper* loading in the dock and I am sure that today, no one would believe that a dock was ever there, or a channel leading to the river.

CHAPTER II

The schooner Alfred *– great gale of November 1890 – a trip to Pentewan – the* Earl of Lathom *– the* Enterprise *– a tide watch*

IN OCTOBER 1890 MY FATHER BECAME MASTER OF THE schooner *Alfred*, of Chester. This vessel was built at Flint and she was quite a good sea boat, and the best command my father had had. Her owner was a Mr. Jones who lived in Chester. My father was very pleased with this vessel, and he took my eldest brother and myself for a trip in her. We joined the ship in the port of Ulverston, where we loaded a cargo of pig iron for Swansea. On leaving, we encountered strong head winds and the forestay sail blew away. This is a very necessary sail for tacking ship. We put into the Mersey and anchored at New Ferry, where we joined about sixty other vessels, all lying weatherbound. There we lay, moored not far from Brunel's fine ship the *Great Eastern*, now being broken up for scrap. My father ordered a new staysail and it was understood that it would be despatched to the railway station without delay.

It was the fifth of November and I remember the day as clearly as if it were yesterday. The strong westerly wind had died away and the day dawned like a fine summer's morning. The sun shone in a cloudless sky and a gentle breeze blew from the south-east. Everyone was happy, for the long miserable spell of lying weather-bound was over, and we could hear the merry voices of the crews, as the anchor chains were hove short. Vessels that had lain here for weeks now got under way, and my father was very upset that he could not sail with them. He and my brother went off in the small boat, to see if by chance the sail had arrived, and finding that it had, collected it, but they did not return until after dark, when every vessel had sailed. As the day wore on the weather began to worsen and it quickly deteriorated. When the boat came alongside with my father and brother bringing the sail, it was raining and blowing hard. During the night, the wind shifted to the north-west and blew with hurricane force. This was remembered for many years, this great November gale of 1890. When the force of wind struck her, our vessel dragged both her anchors and grounded on the sand, very close to the *Great Eastern*, where she did quite a bit of kicking and pounding, which made her strain and leak.

This gale caused great damage and loss of life at sea. Some little vessels were found, their crews dead from exposure. I believe over twenty men from our village lost their lives and several men were lost from the vessels that sailed from New Ferry on that fine autumn morning.

After the storm had died away, my father and I went home for a few days, and on our way we called to see the owner, Mr. Jones. I heard my father relate how the vessel had pounded the bottom when she dragged ashore but he did not mention that they had to use the pumps. After being told about the pounding, Mr. Jones said, 'But she can stand a lot of that, can't she, Captain?' My father did not reply but after we had left the house he remarked to me, 'That's all he knows about how much she can stand.'

Of the rest of the voyage I remember little, until the vessel was in Swansea Bay with the tug boat alongside and the anchor being hove up. There was ice on the barrel of the windlass and the chain was slipping. My father asked me to get a chain and to hook-link it in the cable and when this was done, to hold on. The anchor chain held and the anchor was hove up. My hands were bitterly cold and paining me so much, that I went below to warm them by the cabin fire but this only made them worse. I thought my fingers would burst. My brother came to see how I was and found me crying with the pain. He told me it was a very foolish thing to warm cold fingers by the fire.

We loaded in Swansea for Pentewan, a little port in Cornwall and it was near to Christmastide when we arrived. It was a difficult place for a sailing vessel to enter without some assistance and my father was not sure if there was sufficient water to take us in, so we cruised around for several hours, hoping the boatmen would come to our aid. No one came, so we put back to Falmouth to await the next spring tides.

The able seaman who was one of our crew had given me a pair of sea boots, which I proudly wore although they were a lot too large for me. I thought they were fine and I wore them, thinking that whoever saw me dressed in this manner, would know without doubt that I was a sailor and accept me without any question.

My father had a friend who was master of a fine three masted schooner, called the *Earl of Lathom*[1]. He was fond of children and he took rather more than usual notice of me. He was a fine looking man and as fine a man as he looked. His ship was in Falmouth when we arrived. He came aboard, and when he saw me in my big sea boots, he pretended he wanted to sign me on as a member of his crew. A very serious conference was held in my presence about the conditions attached to joining his ship, wages being the main consideration. It was at last decided that I should be paid ninepence a day and that the engagement should last for one day only. Everything being agreed upon I went aboard with him. He showed me around and told me what he wanted me to do. When he came to the galley, he asked me if I liked sea-pie. Having assured him that I did, he said that one should be made especially for me. When dinner time came I had a place of honour next to him and sea-pie was brought to the table. Everyone made a great fuss of me and in the evening I was taken by boat back to our vessel.

I awoke one morning about a week later and heard the sound of many people walking about the decks. I quickly realised that while I slept we had sailed from Falmouth and were now in the dock in Pentewan. These coasting vessels were very important to the people in these small ports and the arrival of a vessel such as ours was quite an event. As soon as the vessel was alongside, people came aboard, and my father was besieged by a crowd of tradesmen, all soliciting orders, among them the shipbroker's runner, the baker, the butcher, the grocer, the tailor and the ship's chandler. It was an important event when the cargo was discharged, for then the captain received his freight and the crew their wages. Money was sent home, the owner received his share, dock dues and shipstores dealers were paid and everyone was happy but within a few days the vessel would load another cargo, and (as a rule) by that time everyone would be hard up again.

As for me, I went ashore in my sea boots, as good a sailor, I thought, as anyone. My father had sent me to buy some bread. Arriving at the bakehouse I was served by a jolly middle aged woman, who, when she saw me, in my large sea boots, took a fancy to me and gave me a bagful of saffron cakes. I became friendly with her and ran her errands, going around the ships and taking orders for her.

The schooner *Enterprise* was at Pentewan with us, and her master Captain Bithell and the mate his brother, belonged to Flint. They were friends of my father. I remember hearing how on one occasion the *Enterprise* had made a record run to London from Connah's Quay in seventy two hours. She had been at sea in the November gale and had survived.

We were soon loaded and ready to sail again. Before we left I went to the bakehouse to take my leave of the jolly woman. We were talking in the kitchen at the back of the shop and when I told her we were about to sail, she said, 'My little dear, I cannot let you leave me. Will you stay here and live with me always? Will you?' I answered readily, 'Yes, I will'. I heard laughter in the shop and when I looked around, there were the faces of my father and Captain Bithell, grinning at me from the doorway.

We returned to Runcorn and when the vessel arrived I went back to school. In the following March, 1891, there was a severe blizzard, when more disasters occurred and more lives were lost than in the previous November's gale. My father was so long at sea before making harbour that he was given up for lost. At the same time, poor Captain Bithell was lost with all his crew. The Bithells were well liked in the neighbourhood, and Flint church was filled with people who came to pay their respects and to hear Canon Nicholas preach a memorial service from the text 'The sea shall give up its dead.'

I am not sure how long it was after my trip in the *Alfred*, that the owner put the ship up for sale. I remember the vessel was tied up, waiting for a purchaser and she lay in the Georges Dock in Liverpool, near where the Unilever Buildings now stand. I stayed with my father on board her, for a week before she was sold. She lay alongside a barque which was also up for sale. One day being curious to see this barque, I took a long ladder and climbed up to reach her deck. I was met by a watchman who let me walk around the ship and I remember sitting in the galley beside him, watching cockroaches flying around.

One day a buyer came to inspect the vessel. It was well on into the evening when the inspection was over, after which, my father went ashore with this man to have a drink. In those days there was a bye-law, enforced by the Mersey Dock and Harbour Board that a tide watch must be held, the watch being from two hours before high water until one hour after—three hours in all, the person keeping watch, compelled to remain on deck the whole time. This was hard on little vessels with small crews and the police would let no one escape, in fact, they would often try to catch and trap the person keeping watch, by calling in a quiet voice, 'Ship Ahoy', and if an answer was not given, immediately, then the watchman would be accused of being down below and he would be summoned to appear at Dale Street Police Station and he would be fined.

The night my father went ashore with the buyer, the tide watch commenced at 1.00 a.m. and finished at 4.00 a.m. I was not very old and sitting down in the cabin by myself, I was very worried because it was getting late and my father had not come back. I was afraid he would have to pay the fine if he did not keep the tide watch and that was a very serious matter in those days, when there was not much money about.

There was also another bye-law to be observed in which all fires and lights must be extinguished by 11.00 p.m., a fire bell ringing on the docks to warn everyone of the hour. I made sure the fire was out and the light also.

Shortly afterwards, my father came aboard. He had had a few drinks and was slightly intoxicated. From what I have written it seems as if my father was fond of strong drink but this was not so, for he seldom took any, and when he did, it had an adverse effect on him. He came down the cabin and finding that I was still up said,

'Go to bed Hugh.'

'No!' I replied, 'I am going to keep the tide watch.'

'Oh well' he said sleepily, 'if you are going to keep the tide watch, I am going to bed.'

And to bed he went. When the hour came for the tide watch, I went on deck, and it was not long before I heard a policeman call, 'Schooner Ahoy!'

'Hello!' I answered.

'Hello what?' asked the policeman.

'I am keeping the tide watch,' I replied.

He did not ask me any further questions and off he went. He came back again later, at about 3.00 a.m. He called again, 'Schooner Ahoy!'

'Hello!' I answered again, but this time he replied, 'It's all right sonny, you can go to bed now.'

I went below and I crawled over the sleeping figure of my father in his bunk, and I lay between him and the vessel's side. I was soon fast asleep.

A few hours later, I awakened to the sound of men's voices and to the smell of bacon frying. I listened to their voices and I heard my father tell the buyer he was sure he would be fined for he had not kept the tide watch. I put my head out of the bunk and said, 'It's all right, I kept the tide watch.'

My father was astonished. He had no recollection of what had happened the night before. The buyer, who had returned to do business with my father that morning, put his hand into his pocket and gave me a shilling.

The next day we went home, for the schooner was sold.

---

[1] In 1915, she was sunk off the south coast of Ireland by a German U-boat lurking in these waters and waiting for the liner *Lusitania*.

CHAPTER III

A move to Flint in 1895 – soup kitchens – at sea on the Mary Elizabeth *– Limerick – Innishmore – the local magistrate – Mullaghmore – the missing hour – Scotland – 'Go scrape the mast' – in court – the captain's hoard of food*

THIS WAS THE MOST DIFFICULT FEW YEARS OF MY MOTHER'S life. She was the daughter of a sea captain and both my father and my eldest brother were sailors. Her life was one of constant worry and anxiety and this made her determined that my younger brother and I should not go to sea. Anything else was preferable, though we did not share her opinion or her fears.

So we moved to the town of Flint where my mother hoped to find employment for her sons. A more unfortunate time could not have been chosen. The year was 1895, the year of the great frost and a time of the greatest distress and hardship the town had experienced in living memory. The main source of local employment was the Chemical Works, owned by Muspratts. The works had been bought by the United Alkali Company and they dismissed the whole labour force. There was no unemployment benefit in those days and the people were hungry and cold in one of the severest winters on record.

My brother and I started school. I remember, that each day, at eleven thirty a.m. the master would announce: 'All boys whose fathers are out of work are released to go to Cornist Hall for their dinners.'

Although my father was not out of work, my brother and I were released with the others. It did not take us long to walk to the Hall where we were served with a large bowl of steaming hot soup and a piece of bread. Incidentally, the soup at Trelawney Square was not as good as that at Cornist Hall. After this we would go home for dinner. I know this sounds greedy but to my brother and I, young lads as we were, to us it was just fun.

Although my father was never out of work, there was never enough money to go around, so as I grew older, I became anxious to earn a little to help out. My first job was as an errand boy to a grocer. Other jobs followed, for brief periods. I liked none of them. At last, one Saturday afternoon, a friend came to tell me some wonderful news. The schooner *Mary Elizabeth* was loading at Connah's Quay for Limerick and there was a vacancy on board her for a boy cook, and furthermore, the job would be mine if I applied for it on Monday next.

On the following Monday I met the captain of the *Mary Elizabeth* and obtained the berth of cook, at fifteen shillings a month. Now, I was what I had always looked forward to be: a member of a ship's crew. Remembering those happy trips I had made with my father, I looked to the future with great anticipation.

The crew of the *Mary Elizabeth* consisted of the captain and the mate who occupied the cabin aft, an able seaman (A.B.), an ordinary seaman and myself, who occupied the forecastle in the bows.

I went home very excited to tell my mother the good news, feeling I wanted to tell everyone that I was going to sea. One old man to whom I spoke, dolefully remarked; 'Going to sea are you? Well, all I can say . . . . you will get more kicks than ha'pence.' I could not understand why he should make a remark like that.

I joined the ship and we finished loading the cargo before being towed to Wildroads where we anchored. The weather was unsettled, with the wind against us. The captain went home with the pilot, which was the custom with all vessels sailing out of Connah's Quay, the masters staying at home while their vessels remained in Wildroads in charge of a mate.

I soon found out that life on this ship was going to be quite different from when I went on trips with my father. No one on board was interested in me, except the mate, who took an instant dislike to me. Each day, as we lay windbound, he would follow me around the deck, finding fault with everything I did, and one day, he gave me a savage kick which I felt for days.

I was called every morning at 5.00 a.m. to keep anchor watch and to prepare breakfast for 8.00 a.m. I was not allowed below in the forecastle until 8.00 p.m. when I had to wash myself and then turn in my bunk.

Day after day, I would sit in the galley by myself, waiting for the time when I could go below, feeling most homesick and desolate. The mate would amuse himself by getting me out of bed, sometimes at 3.00 a.m. to wash a saucepan which he thought was not clean enough. Used to kindness and affection, I was desperately unhappy at this treatment. The days passed so slowly that I was beginning to think we would remain at anchor for ever.

The change came at last when the wind shifted to the east. The captain came aboard and we got under way. I soon forgot the misery of lying windbound, in the excitement of being on the move. When evening came, although it was my watch below, I stayed on deck, as it was such a delight to see the vessel under way going through the water, until the captain told me I had better go below and get some sleep, as I should be on watch from eight bells midnight till 4.00 a.m.

We had a grand run to the Shannon. There we were towed from Scattery Island to Limerick by a local passenger paddle steamer, and we reached Limerick on a Saturday. I was impatient for the evening to come, as I wanted to see the town. After tea, I watched the A.B. and the ordinary seaman put on their best clothes in readiness for going ashore and then go aft to get a sub on their wages. It was now my turn. I dressed in my best clothes and set off towards the cabin for a sub. Originally I was going to ask the captain for a half crown but having seen his face I thought it wiser to ask for a shilling. The captain had a friend with him in the cabin, a captain from Connah's Quay whose ship was also then in Limerick.

'Well!' said the captain looking at me, 'What do you want and why are you wearing your best clothes?'

'I am going ashore,' I replied, 'and would like a shilling.'

'What do you want a shilling for?' he demanded sternly.

I was now getting confused and replied, foolishly, 'To get some soap.'

'Soap!' he said, and looked at me as if I had taken leave of my senses. 'You go forward and take off those clothes. You will only be allowed ashore on Sunday afternoons, and then, only after you have washed your dinner mugs.'

The captain, however, was not unkind to me, although the mate never missed any opportunity to make my life a misery. Autumn had now set in and I spent my fifteenth birthday in Limerick.

After our cargo was discharged, we chartered to load a cargo of kelp[1] at four different ports: Innishmore, Rutland in the Rosses, Mullaghmore and Buncrana.

Our first loading port was Kilronan, on Innishmore, largest of the Aran Islands in Galway Bay. We were sailing along at a grand rate, at least six knots, approaching the island when we saw a canvas-covered canoe, manned by four strong looking men, who were pulling towards us. They were clothed in short home-spun trousers, knitted jerseys, tam-o-shanter caps and wearing shoes made of rawhide. They passed close to us and dropped astern in our wake. These men had come to put a pilot aboard but the captain was not keen on taking one because of the expense. I heard him say to the mate, 'They will not overtake us at the speed we are going'. However, contrary to his expectations, the boat was soon alongside without effort, the pilotage agreed upon and one of them aboard as pilot at the wheel.

At Innishmore, the Aran islanders took a great interest in our vessel, for it was seldom that one of our size came to the port. Here, incidentally, no coal was ever used, there being an abundance of peat. I thought the smell of burning peat very pleasant, and I obtained some to try in the galley stove. As it burned quite well, I made a fire with it in the cabin, but my efforts did not meet with the captain's approval, for when he came down and smelled the burning peat, he became angry and made me remake it with coal.

I remember going aboard one of the local trading craft called a 'hooker' which was a boat of quite large size. I looked down the open hatch into the cabin below and there saw three men sitting around a peat fire, hardly visible through the smoke. This was escaping through the open hatch, there being no funnel to take it away. The men did not appear to be in any discomfort and I was told that men who sailed in these craft never suffered from any chest complaints.

After leaving Innishmore, we arrived at our next port of call, Rutland in the Rosses, in County Connemara. There we moored to a quay close by a herring curing station. As the season was at its height, there was considerable activity, with Scottish girls gutting, salting and packing the herring into barrels for export.

The man who piloted us to our berth was a fisherman and as we approached his boat he was pulling in a net full of herrings, their scales shining like silver. When we came alongside he asked us for a bucket, which he returned to us filled with freshly caught fish. I shall never forget how much we enjoyed them. After the monotony of coasting sail food, those herrings were manna from Heaven. Our breakfast each morning was either boiled oats or salt fish, with black coffee and ship's biscuits. Coffee was made by putting a couple of spoonsful into the kettle, filling it with water and bringing it to the boil. Sugar was added but no milk although the captain had condensed milk in his. For dinner we had boiled salt beef, potatoes and sometimes a vegetable, but the one thing to which we looked forward was a fine big suet pudding full of currants and raisins which we had on a Sunday. This was the one day of the week when I could honestly say that I had enough to eat. For tea, there were always ship's biscuits and margarine plus tea without milk. If any potatoes were left over from dinner, they were fried and served up hot for tea. There was then nothing more until next morning. When we were in harbour over a weekend, we usually had a couple of loaves of bread. We called this 'soft bread' and it disappeared so quickly that it made the captain gasp when he considered how much it would take to run the ship if 'soft bread' was provided every day.

In this port, the leading merchant was also a local magistrate, with a reputation for being a heavy drinker. Nevertheless, our captain seemed anxious to keep on friendly terms with him, mainly because he was in the kelp business. Consequently, he was invited on board for a midday meal and our captain bought a fine leg of lamb which he told me to cook in readiness for his guest. I cooked the joint and prepared the meal but the guest did not arrive. The captain got tired of waiting and went ashore; then, a couple of hours later, the guest arrived and quite the worse for drink. He was a fine handsome man and well dressed. He asked me, 'Was the captain aboard?' to which I replied, 'He has gone ashore.' He enquired had he been expected and I told him that a dinner had been prepared for him, including a leg of lamb. He then asked was any of the lamb left. I informed him it had not been touched, so he followed me into the cabin, removed his coat and prepared to sample my cooking, while I took the lamb from the cupboard and put it on the table with a loaf of bread. I told him to help himself, while I went to the galley to make him a cup of coffee.

As I was going, he said, 'If you feel in the pocket of my coat you will find my purse. Open it and take what money is in it, you may keep it.' 'What a generous man!' I thought. But when I opened the purse there was only one sixpence there. This I put in my pocket.

I took the coffee down to the cabin where our visitor was enjoying his meal, and the joint looked a sorry sight by the time he had finished with it. Our guest got up from the table; I helped him on with his coat and he went ashore. I did not see him again.

Later, the captain came aboard, and looking in the cupboard in the hope of having a nice meal of cold meat. Being disappointed he got into a furious temper and not knowing what had happened accused me of eating it.

We were now ready to go to sea again and it was near to high water but our pilot failed to turn up. However, our captain decided to sail without him. We had not gone far, when he became confused as to whether or not he was in the right channel. In a state of great anxiety he called out, 'We are in the wrong channel!' We all expected the vessel to strike a rock but nothing happened and we were soon out clear, heading for our next port of call, which was Mullaghmore on the south side of Donegal Bay.

On arrival there, the captain told me to sit in the galley and make sure that no one stole the pots and pans (I don't know what cause he had to think that way) but the moment we moored alongside the quay, we had almost everyone in the place on board the ship. There just wasn't room to move about the deck. I took up my position in the galley but was soon jammed in a corner with as many men as could find room with me, surrounded by as many faces as could peep inside through the window and the door. None of our visitors had any intention of stealing anything, but were curious to see this large schooner which had entered their tiny port.

After taking in this portion of our cargo, we sailed north round Bloody Foreland for our final loading port, Buncrana in Lough Swilly. Arriving here, we completed the loading, left the pier and anchored out in the Lough. It was late in the evening and anchor watches were set. I always kept the last watch so that I could prepare breakfast. I was called at 4.00 a.m. and told to watch that the vessel did not drag her anchor and that the riding light was alight. This particular morning when I was called, I was dreadfully sleepy. The morning was windy and very cold and my first job was to make a fire in the old cast iron ship's stove in the galley. After lighting the fire I shut both galley doors to keep out the cold and as the fire burnt up and warmed the galley, it gave me such a sense of comfort that I stretched myself out on the hard galley seat and went to sleep. When I awoke, feeling cold, I found it was now daylight and the fire in the stove had burned itself out. This morning, it was oatmeal porridge for breakfast, which required cooking for at least half an hour, and my orders were to call the crew at 7.45 a.m. and to have breakfast ready on the table by 8 a.m. prompt. I was in a panic. This would provide a fine excuse for the mate to inflict some punishment on me.

I had to find out the time. The only clock in the ship was in the cabin but the time could be seen by looking into the cabin from the deck through the skylight. I was astonished to discover it was exactly eight o'clock. I quietly crept down the cabin stairs, got on the table and put the hands of the clock back one hour. Then, quickly I returned to the deck, without disturbing either the captain or the mate; although in my mind there was the possibility that the captain on waking might look at his watch.

I hastily remade the fire and as there was a good draught it burned up quickly. I put the porridge saucepan on the stove and as soon as the water came to the boil put enough oatmeal in it to thicken without having to cook it the half hour. I then removed the pan and put on the kettle. As soon as it boiled I crept aft again and finding that it was now 7.45 a.m. (by the clock) I called the mate and then ran forward to call the crew.

Breakfast was on the table and we began our meal. The mate tasted his porridge, glared at me and asked in a rough voice, 'How long have you boiled this porridge? It isn't cooked.' I replied that I had boiled it for half an hour. Fortunately no one else made any protests and I escaped very well out of this situation and during the day the clock (with my assistance) caught up the missing hour.

We were bound with our full cargo of kelp for Queensborough in Kent, and before leaving Buncrana we took a lot of fresh vegetables aboard together with a quantity of fresh beef, and were thus well stocked up, making a big improvement in our food situation.

We sailed through Innistrahull Sound and next day at noon passed Belfast Lough. It was Sunday and I well remember the fine dinner we had that day. When the captain, mate and able seaman had had their dinner, the ordinary seaman and I went below for ours: fresh roast beef and vegetables and a large suet pudding to follow. The beef and vegetables tasted so good, that I decided I could manage a second helping before starting on the 'duff' (our name for the pudding), when to my dismay the ordinary seaman put all this on his plate.

'Aren't you going to give me any?' I asked.

'No' he replied, 'You've had enough dinner already.'

Not to have a portion of that 'duff' was too dreadful to contemplate, so I went on deck and told the captain what had happened. He came down the cabin and seeing this large helping of pudding on the ordinary seaman's plate, he picked up a fork, stuck it in the 'duff' and put it on my plate; at the same time telling him he was 'a greedy b——r.'

When I had finished my meal and returned on deck, the captain asked me if I had eaten the lot. When I said that I had, he remarked, 'You are a b——y cormorant!'

Next day, the weather being unsettled, we put in to Holyhead harbour for shelter. As there was no prospect of any improvement in the weather, the captain moored the *Mary Elizabeth* with both anchors and went home, leaving the mate in charge. I was not happy to see the captain go, as the thought of being left with the mate was not a cheerful one. As soon as the captain had gone, the mate began to harass me. Lying windbound in a schooner in the winter, with short days and very little to do to occupy the time, is a most monotonous experience. My life became so miserable that at times I felt ready to try and swim ashore. At last, one day, the able seaman who was a big powerful man, told the mate to stop tormenting me, and furthermore, warned him that if he was looking for trouble, he (the able seaman) would oblige him. The mate assured him blandly that he had no desire to be anything but good friends with everyone, and so things were a little better for me after that.

The weather fined up, and our captain returned from home. As soon as he came aboard, the mate informed him that he was leaving the ship and asked to be paid off. The captain was furious and refused to release him. All crews joining coasters had to sign articles of agreement, accepting conditions. They were all paid monthly and had free food. In the articles it was clearly stated that no one could leave ship in a windbound port, and twenty four hours notice of leave must be given, which would only be accepted at the final port of discharge of cargo.

Our captain was particularly angry because all the other vessels which had been with us, waiting for this fair wind, were under way, and we would be unable to sail if the mate insisted on being paid off. I listened by the skylight to the angry voices below of the captain and the mate, and I was hoping the captain would settle a few old scores for me. But the quarrel did not go as far as that, and the main thing, as far as I was concerned, was to see the mate clear off the ship. Well, the mate actually did defy the captain and he deserted the *Mary Elizabeth*. As we could not sail without a mate, we remained at anchor until a few days later we shipped another mate. We sailed at last with a strong east wind. This gave us a hard beat up from the Longships off Land's End to Falmouth, where we put in for shelter until the wind shifted to the west. At last we arrived at Queensborough. It was January 1896 when we discharged; we had been a long time over one cargo.

We loaded then at Rochester with a cargo of cement for Oban and Fort William. The trip in contrast to the last one was a good one and we did it in record time, exactly seven days. It was a long run by sea and the wind was strong, dead aft most of the way. Our schooner, the *Mary Elizabeth*, was a two-masted vessel with a main boom of fifty feet and with that slacked out to the full length of the main sheet, plus a gaff topsail set over the big mainsail, it required the utmost skill on the part of the helmsman not to gybe that big sail over. I stayed close to him and watched the water passing under the big sail in a mass of white foam, the vessel doing nine knots. Miscalculation on the part of the helmsman could have torn the mast out. In this manner we passed through the Sound of Islay. I remember the captain was so pleased with this quick run that we had 'soft bread' for tea to mark the occasion.

After discharging, we left Fort William bound in ballast for Connah's Quay. We had not gone far through the narrow waters, when the wind came ahead. We anchored in a lovely stretch of water at the foot of Ben Nevis. The weather was very frosty and one bitterly cold morning the captain called from his bed berth to ask me what work the crew were engaged upon. I told him I believed they were still in the forecastle. I knew it would be warm there.

'Well,' the captain said, 'tell them to get the scraping knives and scrape the masts.'

I was privately of the opinion that it was too cold for anyone to be strung aloft scraping masts but I went forward and gave the message. The crew laughed when I told them, and said, 'Go, tell the old man if he wants the masts scraped to get on with it himself.'

When I returned aft, the captain asked me had they got the knives out and on hearing they had refused to do the job, he got out of his bunk, slipped on his trousers, put on a pair of slippers and went forrard. I followed him as he went down the forecastle and I heard him ask the crew did they think he paid them wages to sit around the fire all day. The only answer he got in reply, was a laugh that infuriated him so much, that he took hold of the stove pipe, unshipped it and smashed it on the forecastle floor.

'There!' he said, 'if you won't work you shall have no fire.'

A flow of language accompanied the captain as he came up the ladder to the deck. He was followed by the able seaman who was using dreadful language and offering to fight. The captain, a fine big man, turned around and hit him one blow and he fell to the deck unconscious.

I thought he had killed him and asked should I get some water. 'No!' replied the captain, 'throw the b——d overboard.'

It was not long before the able seaman came to. He got up and went below, moaning. Listening to those dismal groans coming from below, the captain, his temper now quite gone, went down to the able seaman to tell him how sorry he was that he had hurt him so badly and to advise him to lie down in his bunk and to take it easy. But the more the captain sympathised with him the louder he groaned, until all the captain's good intentions vanished and he became quite as angry as before. He now accused the man of shamming and threatened him that for two pins he would give him another blow to put him straight. He then left the forecastle. Shortly afterwards, the able seaman stopped moaning. Taking a sheath knife in his hand he came on deck, calling out as he went towards the cabin.

'Come on deck, you old so and so, and I'll cut your heart out!'

The captain, hearing him, was on deck before the able seaman reached the cabin. He had a revolver in his hand and told the seaman that if he came one step further, he would shoot. Then the captain came to a sudden decision. He would pay this trouble maker off and he told him so.

'Do that,' said the able seaman.

The ordinary seaman who was on deck, said, 'Yes, and me too. Give me my wages.' So both signed off the articles, were paid up to date and landed on the shore with their belongings.

We were now only three left to man the ship and so we returned to Fort William to get more men as crew. We got back in the evening and anchored off the town. At two o'clock in the morning, we were awakened by the police, who had come off in their boat, to arrest our captain. They had a warrant for his arrest, on a charge of assault on a defenceless member of his crew, with an iron bar.

The mate and I followed the police boat ashore in our ship's boat. After some time at the police station, the captain was allowed to return to the *Mary Elizabeth* on bail, to appear at eleven o'clock the same morning to answer the charge.

The three of us from the ship were at the court in good time. The able seaman and the ordinary seaman were already in their seats, and they looked very pathetic. By the time they had given their evidence the court had adjourned for lunch. The captain took the mate and I to a restaurant where we each had a plateful of ham with bread and butter. The waiter placed a plateful of fancy cakes in the centre of the table and they looked very tempting to us. When we had finished our meal, there were still some cakes left on the plate, so I put them into a bag and took them back to the court, the captain paying the bill without question.

When the court resumed, things began to look very black for the captain, for the evidence was not going at all in his favour. When I entered the witness box, the man who was questioning me, asked, was it not a fact that the captain was a violent man and had he not treated me harshly? To this I replied, quite truthfully, that this was not so, he had never treated me harshly. He implied that the captain had bought me a bag of cakes to induce me to answer in his favour, and then asked me, 'Did I not think it a terrible thing that the captain had struck this poor man with an iron bar?'

I replied: 'If the captain had done so, he would have killed him.'

His reply to this was that other witnesses had stated that the captain had used the iron bar. To which I made answer, 'As I was the only one on deck when the incident happened, it was not possible for anyone else to give reliable evidence.' In addition to this I affirmed, 'If the captain, who was justly infuriated by the filthy names the able seaman had called him, had used an iron bar, then surely death would have resulted.' Following this, after a short consultation, the captain was fined one pound. After paying this fine, and as soon as we were outside the court, the captain said to me, 'My God, Hugh, had it not been for you, I would have been sent to prison for a month.'

Soon afterwards, the captain went home, after telling us that he would send two retired captains to make the trip home to Connah's Quay. It was several days before our new shipmates arrived, and the mate being in charge, set about tidying the cupboards in the cabin. He came upon a small hoard of food and called me to come and see it. He was quite excited with what he had found. There was (to begin with) a couple of pounds of fresh butter; which we hadn't tasted since we had joined the vessel. There were a dozen tins of condensed milk, bottles of lemon squash, several tins of sweet biscuits, a dozen eggs and several other things of which we were fond. The mate said to me, 'We won't let the new arrivals know anything of what we have found; we will have the lot for ourselves.' I helped him remove the food to a safer place, and in a few days time the two captains arrived.

We were soon back at Connah's Quay, the two captains were paid off and our own captain once again in charge. I was in the cabin when the captain was searching through the cupboards. He asked me had I seen anything of any tins of biscuits, and when I appeared not to understand what he was talking about, he muttered to himself, 'The greedy old b——s have eaten the lot.'

By this time, I thought I would look for another ship, and although the captain offered me a rise of five shillings, bringing my wages to a pound a month, I gave in my notice and left.

---

[1] Kelp is a black greasy substance made from seaweed burnt in quantity for the potash, iodine, etc., that they contain.

CHAPTER IV

The Emma and Esther – *the* Not Forgot – *cargoes for Ireland – the* Lizzie *– from Gravesend with a cargo of explosives – ordinary seaman on the* Sunbeam *– the* Elizabeth Hyam *– the* Hilda *– I join the* Victor *as mate – an unsound vessel – the* Isabella

I MUST GO BACK A LITTLE NOW TO WHEN I WAS VERY young. My father had a particular friend, who was master and part owner of the schooner *Emma and Esther*. He was a man greatly respected by everyone. He lived in the country, close to us, and often called to see my father when he was at home. He would often give me a penny and jokingly ask me 'When was I going to join his ship as cook?'

A day or so after I left the *Mary Elizabeth*, someone told me that Captain Lloyd (my father's friend) had a vacancy aboard the *Emma and Esther* for a cook. That was great news to me, for he was the one captain with whom I wanted to sail, and I thought he would like to have me as his cook.

I met him on the quay and asked him for the berth but he did not appear to be at all excited over shipping me. 'Are you a good cook?' he asked me. 'I can steer, splice and scull a boat,' I replied. 'I asked you,' he said, 'can you cook?' When I assured him that I could, he took me aboard his ship and showed me the galley. 'Can you keep it as tidy as it is now?' he asked, to which I replied, 'Call this tidy? It wants a good clean up.' We proceeded through the cabin cupboards with the same questions and he told me, if I could keep up the same state of tidiness, this was all that would be required of me.

Many times after I had joined his ship, Captain Lloyd would look in the galley and exclaim, 'What I am paying this fellow thirty shillings a month for, I do not know.'

I was in constant trouble for such things as chopping wood on deck without a chopping block, losing draw buckets and cutlery over the ship's side, only remembering the cutlery was still in the bucket after its contents had been emptied over the side.

The mate of the *Emma and Esther* was an inoffensive old Welshman, and I, after having been kept under so strictly by the first mate with whom I sailed, found that I could have fine fun playing tricks on him. He behaved like a baby and told the captain everything I did, until the latter became thoroughly tired of hearing about my misdeeds. Furthermore, he constantly implored the captain to take me in hand, but all Captain Lloyd did was to threaten me with some dreadful punishment if I did not mend my ways.

One day, I was serving up some fried potatoes for our tea, when a mischievous idea occurred to me. I picked up the pepper pot and put a generous sprinkling of pepper on the mate's portion. We all took our places at table and I, keeping a straight face, awaited results. Captain Lloyd was a dignified, reserved man and our meals were always eaten in silence; we had too much respect for him to indulge in conversation. The mate, after putting some potato in his mouth, let out a cry, shattering the silence and actually making the captain jump. The captain glared at the mate and asked him in a sharp voice. 'Whatever is the matter with you?' 'Cap'n,' the mate gulped, as he washed the hot potato down his throat with near boiling tea, 'Cap'n, this bloody lad has put so much pepper in the potatoes it has burned my throat.'

The captain carefully sampled his portion and then, looking severely at the mate said, 'I don't know what has come over you; of course there isn't too much pepper. Get your tea and stop making such a fuss.' So the silly mate ate the remainder of his portion with a gulp at every swallow.

On a later occasion, after a series of pranks on the poor defenceless mate, an incident occurred which brought things to a head and led to another change in my seafaring career. We had put into Newlyn for shelter and the able seaman and the ordinary seaman were ashore. I was in the forecastle by myself. The mate called to me from the scuttle, 'Have you put any meat in soak?' 'Yes' I replied. I had put a piece of meat in soak, but really it was more bone than meat. When the mate saw it he said, 'Do you call that a piece of meat? Put another piece in.' I went to the cask with another piece of meat and as I passed by the mate, I muttered, 'There is always something wrong with you.' 'What did you say?' he asked. 'There is always something wrong on this ship.' 'You did not,' he rejoined, 'you said me.' At this time I was going down the forecastle steps. With that he said, 'For two pins I will come down with you.' I replied, 'Yes, you come down.'

So down he came. I was now a little scared and I picked up the poker, as I thought to defend myself with. As soon as the mate saw the poker in my hand, he raced back up the ladder calling out as he ran, 'Cap'n! Cap'n! This bloody lad has turned on me at last!'

It was a dark night and I thought, 'The best place for me now is on the quay.' I had a great liking and respect for Captain Lloyd but with constant complaints from the mate, I was sure if he got hold of me he would give me a good shaking. It was not long before I saw him come from the cabin and march along the deck in a determined manner; go to the forecastle and call out in an angry voice, 'Come up here.'

He called again when there was no reply and said, 'If you don't come up I will come down to you.' Down he went and then back on deck again, still calling, I answered from the quay. 'I am here.' 'Come aboard at once.' he called. I did not obey or answer.

'You young scamp,' he said 'Take your notice and the moment we dock at Runcorn you leave this ship. I will not be pestered with you any longer.'

On arrival there a day or two later I thought I would take the initiative and tell him I am leaving.

'Leaving are you?' Captain Lloyd replied. 'I should think you are.' And that was the end of my brief career on the *Emma and Esther*.

My next berth was in an old schooner smaller than those I had already sailed which carried only a hundred tons. She was called the *Not Forgot*. I shall certainly never forget her. Her crew consisted of the captain, the mate and myself, (the cook). The captain belonged to Flint and though a kindly, superior man had never done very well financially.

My first trip we loaded a cargo of bricks for Dublin at Connah's Quay. It was December and the weather was unsettled, making it necessary for us to anchor in Wildroads. The captain went home as usual. The weather fined up at last, with a light easterly wind and our captain duly returned. The vessels that had been lying with us got under way and the mate and I were expecting to sail with them, when the captain came on deck and said we could not sail until he got some money from the owners to buy provisions. We had practically no food aboard, in fact, only about half a loaf of bread and no potatoes or ship's biscuits. But the mate and I did not want to miss this fair wind, so we persuaded the captain to sail with the other vessels.

The fair wind lasted until next day by which time we were half way across from Holyhead, then the wind died out and fog settled down. All night we lay becalmed. We were now anxious to get to Dublin simply because we had nothing to eat. At daylight a little breeze sprang up and we were able to make Dublin Bay. We came in close to the Poolbeg lighthouse, to await the tug to tow us up the Liffey. We picked up the pilot, who would remain on board until our vessel berthed in Dublin. He was astonished when he found we had no food at all on board. As night came on, the fog settled down again and all night long we heard the doleful sound of the Poolbeg fog signal, with its dismal high and low pitched notes. We were all so hungry by the following morning, the pilot sailed the vessel into Kingston harbour to enable us to buy something to eat. Here the poor captain had no money until the pilot loaned him five shillings. At last we came alongside the quay in Dublin, and the vessel looked so old and decrepit that some men standing on the quay said jokingly to the captain, 'Did he stay out all night in that ship?'

The *Not Forgot* did indeed look a sorry sight, and a couple of days later a Board of Trade inspector came aboard, after an inspection and condemned her for repairs. The mate and I were paid off and I went home by passenger boat. What happened to the old *Not Forgot* I do not know.

After a few days at home, I joined the schooner *Lizzie* as an ordinary seaman, at two pounds ten shillings a month. She was loaded with fireclay goods for Belfast and as the wind and weather were not favourable, we anchored in Wildroads, after towing there from Connah's Quay, the captain going home as usual.

After tea on the same day we paid a visit to some friends who were in a schooner which had anchored in the roads a few days before us. When we got on board, the crew had an exciting story to tell us of a wrecking adventure they had been engaged upon. Some time previously, a large steamer had grounded entering Mostyn and had broken in two. No one was aboard her, for the owners had left the ship to the underwriters and they had refused to accept liability, as the captain had not employed a tugboat.

Our friends showed us a lot of gear they had brought away from the wreck, and it seemed to us that it would be fun to go aboard after dark and see what we too could find. Our friends assured us it would be quite all right to take what was there and we did not need much persuading.

We set off and boarded the wreck, which was full of water, with rats scuttling everywhere. What we brought away was not in fact of much value but it was an exciting adventure.

When we arrived in Belfast, the mate sold what we had taken from the wreck for a few shillings, giving me my share with which I bought a second-hand fiddle—I do not know why as I had no knowledge of music or fiddles. The mate believed he could play any musical instrument, as he could get a tune from a tin whistle and could play the accordion fairly well by ear. When he saw my fiddle he said, 'I'll bet I can get a tune out of that.'

He spent several hours practising, then asked me to listen and see if I could recognise what tune he was supposed to be playing. It only sounded to me like screeching, made by someone rubbing a finger on a pane of glass. The mate got impatient with me: 'Listen again,' he said, and once again scraped the bow across the strings, with the same sounds as before. Eventually, he told me the tune he was playing was 'The Blind Irish Girl' and I had to take his word for it.

We returned in ballast from Belfast and arrived in Wildroads. My father and my eldest brother, whose vessel was also anchored there, came aboard to see me. As soon as they had greeted me, I spoke to my brother and told him I had bought a fiddle. He asked me could I play it. 'No' said I, 'but the mate can.'

I went below and brought up my new purchase, and I asked the mate to show us how well he could play. He had hardly begun, when he stopped playing in amazement at the sight of my brother doubled up with laughter, and he demanded to know what he was laughing at.

'Well' laughed my brother, 'there is no bridge on the fiddle.' Neither the mate nor I knew that a bridge was a necessary part of a fiddle.

We traded in the *Lizzie* from the Bristol Channel to Guernsey and London and back, mostly with scrap iron. I did not remain long in her and my last voyage in her was nearly my last trip of all. It was at Christmastime in 1897, when we sailed from Gravesend with a cargo of cement and ten tons of explosives for Douglas in the Isle of Man. We had light winds as far as Start Point in south Devon which we reached on Christmas Day. Then the wind went southerly, with a falling barometer. The wind steadily increased by the time we reached the Lizard and after passing the Longships, it backed to the south west, and was soon at gale force. We reduced sail until the *Lizzie* was running under bare poles. Looking astern at the great walls of water rolling up, which appeared about to break aboard at any moment, and with the screaming of the gale, I wondered what would be the outcome.

After running for about a hundred miles in these conditions, at about midnight, a great wave broke over the wheelhouse and filled our decks from stem to stern. It was a marvel the old schooner did not sink under the weight of water on her deck and it was a miracle that another sea did not follow. As the water slowly cleared we could see some bulwarks had been washed away, which helped the vessel to get clear of the weight of water. It was now evident that the *Lizzie* had to be brought to, and the double reefed mainsail set. A favourable opportunity to hoist it came and the vessel was brought into the wind and the sail set. With the heavy cargo and the terrible straining, she had begun to leak badly and we had to keep both hand pumps going to keep the water under. After hours of this exhausting work, I do not think any of us would have cared much if the vessel had sunk.

The next afternoon, the wind moderated and we set all sail. After sighting the Codling lightship off the Wicklow coast we kept away for the Isle of Man and the following morning dropped anchor in the pool at Douglas. But before we could enter the harbour, our ten tons of explosives had to be landed. This had to be done without any help from the shore. We took the kegs and boxes of explosives from the hold, put them in the ship's boat, rowed them ashore, then handed them to the carters, and back again until the whole ten tons were landed. It was a long and weary day's work as we were wet and exhausted from lack of sleep and the severity of the trip. It was midnight when we moored alongside the quay; we turned in to sleep in wet bunks, still in our wet clothes and we slept for hours. On this occasion when the cement was discharged, a third of it was found to have been damaged by salt water.

From Douglas we went home empty to Connah's Quay, where I signed off. My clothes were in a sorry state. After dressing in what had been my best clothes I was ashamed to be seen, for everything I had to wear was in the forecastle and had been washed about and soaked with salt water. Two pounds ten shillings a month did not allow for many new clothes. I must have looked a scarecrow. I thought when I got home what a blessing it was to have a home and loving parents to whom I could come when things were not good.

At this time, my father had lost his command and was mate of the schooner *Sunbeam*. She was a fine looking three-masted schooner, with a topsail and standing gallant sail, also a maintopmast staysail. She had finished her trading to Newfoundland and had recently been purchased by the Renays, principal owners of merchant schooners in Connah's Quay. My father and I became shipmates when I shipped in her as ordinary seaman, at the same rate of pay as my last berth, that is two pounds ten a month. But my father was not happy as mate and found it hard to take orders after being in command. It was always a matter of great concern to me that my father should captain his own ship, and it was an occasion of immense satisfaction, when, having sailed together for only two months, a telegram came for him offering him the captain's berth in the schooner *Elizabeth Hyam*.

I was curious to know what sort of vessel this was and how many tons of cargo she could carry. I also wondered if I should be one of her crew. My father knew the vessel and he told me she was only a small craft, but there was the prospect of being able to earn more money as she was to be sailed by the share system. My two brothers would be her crew and I was to stay in my present vessel. I did not really mind, for my father, of whom I thought so much, was going to be in charge again, and to me it was as good as being left a fortune.

This move proved to be a turning point in our fortunes, for my father pleased the owners so much with his care of the *Elizabeth Hyam* and by making quick passages, that after less than two years they made him master of their finest ship, the *Hilda*. She was a schooner, built to their orders by Fergusson and Baird, and named after the owner's daughter, Hilda Hancock of Buckley, in Flintshire.

I remained in the *Sunbeam* for some time. Later I joined my father in the *Hilda*. While in the *Sunbeam* we loaded a cargo of fireclay goods at Connah's Quay for Limerick. When we arrived, the town was celebrating the centenary of the 1798 Rebellion. I remember there was a torchlight procession there and tar barrels burned in the streets.

From Limerick we came back to Swansea, taking three weeks over the trip, being at sea the whole time with light winds ahead. From Swansea we went to Faversham, which was another three weeks passage. I remember towing to Faversham behind a paddle tug up the winding river, through lovely scenery. From there we towed to Cliff Creek, to load cement for Douglas (Isle of Man) and from there we returned to Connah's Quay, where I signed off and joined my father in the *Hilda*.

Now, this was going to sea as I imagined it could be. Good food and the companionship of people of whom you were fond. It is pleasant to look back to this happy time.

My father had in fact done so well since he had taken charge of the *Elizabeth Hyam* that my parents built a new house in Flint. My mother insisted on calling this 'Hyam House' as she considered it was through the good fortune the little vessel had brought us, that it was possible to build this house.

We were doing well in the *Hilda* too and to be on a new ship was such a delight to us that we kept her looking just like a yacht. Indeed she caught everyone's eye. Unfortunately this proved to be our undoing, for someone offered to purchase her at a higher price than she had cost her owners to build, so she was sold and we were all without a ship again.

I next joined the schooner *Victor* as mate. My younger brother William and the young man who was our cook on the *Hilda* formed the remainder of the crew. The *Victor* was a slow, leaky old schooner, built in Scotland, a good sea boat but a poor sailer. The captain had just joined and it was his first command. We thought it was too bad that we had to leave our fine new ship, and accept berths on this worn out old craft. Although we made several trips in her, there was no pleasure and no prospects of improvement in her. We felt sure the captain would not make enough money to pay us our wages when the time came to settle up.

One trip stands out in my memory. We loaded whitening in the Sussex port of Newhaven for Preston. It was a fine summer with calm weather and the vessel being a slow sailer, we were three weeks at sea before having to seek shelter for a time in Wildroads. We had left Newhaven with a very small quantity of fresh food, so that after being at sea for a few days our only food was hard ship's biscuits, poor quality margarine and tea without milk, and this for every meal. We had plenty of ship's biscuits, in fact we had two hundredweight of them, and two large tins of margarine. Like most men who sailed in this type of craft, we accepted these conditions, however, as the fortunes of our trade and very rarely did anyone complain.

After a long spell of quiet calm weather, just after we had passed Holyhead, the wind began to blow very hard from the west. The captain decided that he would put into Wildroads and it was not long after we had anchored when the tug boat *Albert* passed close to us on her way up-river to Connah's Quay. Our captain hailed her and asked for a passage in her to Connah's Quay. The tug boat came alongside, the captain jumped aboard, and we were left to our three selves and the biscuits and margarine. Next day, my brother and our cook, Tom Jones, were engaged in cleaning out the forecastle while I was busy doing something about the deck. My brother came up from the forecastle in a hurry, quite excited; he had found a half crown while cleaning out a locker. This was a great piece of luck for we could not raise a penny piece between us. From where we were anchored, Mostyn village was but a mile away. My brother and I set off in our ship's boat. We bought a seven and a half pound loaf for sevenpence halfpenny, twenty cigarettes for fivepence halfpenny, a pound of butter for ninepence and a large bag full of fruit scones for a few pence. When we got back to our ship's boat, the tide had ebbed and left her dry on the bottom and we had to wait a couple of hours until the tide refloated her. It was getting dark by the time we got back to our ship. After the cook had taken the boat's painter and we had hauled the boat up on the deck, he told us that while we were ashore he had had a stroke of good luck, having obtained a bucketful of flatfish from a fisherman in exchange for a bucketful of salt; he had fried them and they were now ready for us to eat. However long I live, I shall never enjoy a meal more than that one.

Within a few days, the captain returned to us on the *Victor*, bringing his wife with him, to make the trip to Preston. They brought a lot of food with them. The weather having taken a fine turn, we were soon off Preston Bar. As it was calm, the captain did not intend to engage a pilot but he believed it was necessary to take the tug boat, which we could see at some distance away. The captain ordered my brother to take the Union Jack aloft and to make it fast to the foretopmast. (There being no signal halliards on the foremast). The captain's wife was on deck, standing close to her husband, when I spoke to the captain.

'I thought, Skipper, that you did not require the services of a pilot.'

'I do not' he replied.

'Well' I remarked, 'the Union Jack is hoisted on the foremast and that is the signal for a pilot.'

'Nonsense,' he said, 'where would I hoist it if not on the foremast?'

My reply was that the signal for a tug is hoisted on the mainmast. (The signal for a tug is really the burgee hoisted on the mainmast, failing that, some other flag).

The captain's wife said to her husband. 'Why not listen to what he says?'

'Do you think I do not know my job?' was his reply.

The tug boat came alongside bringing the pilot, who jumped aboard. He greeted the captain, informing him that he was the pilot. The captain replied that he did not require him.

'Captain,' the pilot said, 'you are flying the pilot flag, so I remain on board.'

This error cost the captain three pounds and worse still, his wife reminded him of his foolishness in not listening to my advice.

I now received good news from home. My father had been given command of the schooner *Isabella*, a fine fast sailer and a good one in which to get a living. He needed a crew and wished to have myself, my brother and Tom Jones our cook, to sail with him. My brother and cook signed off on hearing this news, and went to join my father. The captain was very distressed to lose them and pleaded with me not to leave him. Feeling sorry for him I agreed to stay. I was beginning to think that my captain was well on the way to becoming one of the unsuccessful captains whom I mentioned earlier. He was only able to ship an able seaman, so we were without a cook when we sailed from Preston with a cargo of coal for Saltash.

During the trip, I had the watch to myself, having to steer the full four hours, and when that time was up, I spent about an hour pumping out the old vessel which was leaking like a sieve. While I was pumping, I called myself a fool for remaining in this leaky old *Victor*. By the time we reached the Bishop lighthouse, it was blowing hard from the east south east. I thought it would been have advisable to have sought shelter before this in Milford until the wind had eased. The vessel had a big mainsail which was double reefed and we were under small canvas, being a two masted schooner. As we were pitching into the sea, the Captain came to me and asked my opinion, should we return to Milford or should we carry on. I told him what I thought, but added that as he was the captain it was for him to decide. 'Right!' he said, 'we will carry on.'

It was my watch until midnight, and I had the deck to myself when the mainsail split from double reef carling right across to the mast. I called the captain and we lowered down the torn sail. There was no alternative but to run before the wind, and make for Waterford. All this time, the *Victor* was taking in water at eight inches an hour, which had to be pumped out with only three of us to do the pumping. We were lucky to make the Hook Light at Waterford without any further trouble and came to anchor in Passage East. Then followed days sitting on deck stitching canvas, repairing the mainsail and pumping out the water.

When the weather improved, we sailed again. Our mainsail was repaired and some of the leaks were stopped, but the *Victor* was still making water at about six inches an hour. We made a good run to Plymouth Sound and while discharging at Saltash the captain fixed us to load heavy scrap for Hull. There was no sign whatever of any repairs being made to the ship, so I gave in my notice to leave. The captain again pleaded with me to stay but this time I made him an offer—to forfeit my six weeks wages to compensate him for my loss, and this he accepted.

Soon I was back again with my father. What a change! A well found, fast sailing vessel and with my own people again.

I should like to mention one trip we made empty from Wexford to Connah's Quay. The weather had been exceptionally stormy, then it calmed down awhile and we had sailed. During the night the gale sprung up again, with heavy rain. It was a very dark night and at the height of the storm 'St. Elmo's Lights' appeared on the mast heads and yard arms. It is a peculiar sight to see these phosphorescent balls of light glowing in the darkness. I have seen this phenomenon several times since that time and have noticed that they always appear at the height of a storm, but very soon afterwards the weather moderates, so really they are a welcome sight.

My elder brother Tom had become captain of my father's old ship, the *Elizabeth Hyam* and he too was doing well. He was in need of a mate so I left the *Isabella* to join him in the *Elizabeth Hyam*.

Our trading was mostly to Ireland, carrying fire-clay goods for the owners. About a year after I had joined my brother, he was offered a larger vessel with the same firm. He accepted and left to join his new command, leaving me aboard with the cook. Our vessel was not covered by insurance so that anyone going master of her did not have to pass a seamanship examination. We were at this time loading potatoes in bulk in the Ulster port of Downpatrick in Strangford Lough, for Liverpool. Several days passed without any word from the owners and then I received a telegram from them, asking me to take charge and they asked for my acceptance ... I accepted.

CHAPTER V

Well here I was, Captain – the Elizabeth Hyam *– Uncle Tom as Mate – the Races – Menai Straits – the frightened mate – the lost anchor at Barrow – a cargo for Cemlyn Bay*

WELL, HERE I WAS, CAPTAIN AND THE DATE I TOOK charge was the thirteenth of March 1904. The *Elizabeth Hyam* was nothing to boast about, but here was an opportunity to prove whether or not I could make the vessel pay a dividend and provide myself with a better living.

My first problem was to find a mate and this difficulty was solved by my father, who had on his crew my mother's brother, who was an experienced coaster and had been master of several vessels. Unfortunately he had a failing, inasmuch as he would take to drink and go on sudden prolonged sprees. For months he would remain strictly teetotal and then without any warning would start on a drinking spree, and would not stop as long as he could raise the price of another drink. Then, when the spree was over, he would be strictly teetotal for such a long time that his friends would think he was cured; yet sooner or later he would start drinking again.

At this time, he was down on his luck and had accepted a berth with my father in the *Isabella*. My father thought, if I had my uncle with me, it would be an added assurance of my safety, and so my Uncle Tom landed aboard. I was pleased to have him with me for he was good company when he was sober, and he always was a lively and intelligent man. The day he came, he spoke to me about drink, earnestly assuring me that he was never really fond of it. It was, he said, just the bad company that started him drinking. He could not understand how anyone could be so foolish as to work hard and save, and then waste it all on drinking. He had no patience with people who did that.

The next morning at breakfast, my uncle expressed a wish to have a ride in an Irish jaunting car and to be driven in one of them to the races, which were taking place in Downpatrick on that day. I agreed it was a good idea, and after breakfast I went to Downpatrick and arranged with a driver to be at the vessel at two in the afternoon.

We dressed in our best clothes, got into the jaunting car and arrived at the field where the races were held. Racing had started but no one seemed very interested in it for the majority of those present were crowding into a large marquee, and those who could not find room inside were grouped around outside, drinking large glasses of creamy stout and making a real day of it.

My uncle could not keep his eyes off those thirsty people. At last he said to me, 'Confound it! What is making me so thirsty? If we had had anything salty for breakfast I could understand it. I don't think I ever felt so thirsty in my life. Do you mind if I go and have a bottle of ginger beer?'

'No,' I said, 'if you are thirsty why not go and get one?'

The ginger beer I am sure was black with a creamy top!

Within a few days, loading was completed and we sailed. After we reached the Anglesey coast it was misty and wet, with a strong easterly wind and I thought it advisable to seek shelter for the night in the Menai Straits. The entrance to the Straits, between Puffin Island and the mainland, is very narrow and with the head wind it was difficult to enter. I mentioned this to my uncle, who said there was no need to enter this channel as we could use the one on the east side of Puffin Island. He offered to take the vessel in for me and I let him take the helm. As we approached the island, he pointed out to me a tower with a square hole near the top and he said that if, as we approached the tower we kept the hole in sight, we should be in the deepest water. We did as he said and came to anchor without trouble. Selfishly, I did not feel too happy that my uncle had navigated the channel without my help, and I did not feel grateful to him. I was very young!

We got under way next day with the wind still ahead but we got as far as the Bar Lightship off the Mersey, where we anchored, over the ebb tide. When the flood tide made, we hove up the anchor. The wind was still easterly and it was misty with a fresh wind, which meant we had to tack up the narrow channel from side to side, to look out for steamers and to make sure not to foul any of the numerous buoys marking each side of the channel. It required a lot of skill and knowledge of the channel and the tide to keep out of trouble. My uncle took charge, as a matter of course, calling 'Ready about' when we were far enough in the channel.

I would ease off the jib sheets and around the vessel would come on the other tack, with a buoy just coming into view and the tide swaying it about. If the vessel had got across one of those big iron buoys she would have sunk. My clever old uncle knew just the right time to tack ship. It was daylight when he skilfully put the vessel alongside the pierhead at Canning Dock, just above the landing stage. I was relieved and glad he was in charge, but at the back of my mind I thought this was no good for I was not really the 'skipper'. I made up my mind that when we arrived and in the future I would take charge whether I came to grief or not.

After discharging our cargo of potatoes, we had to load a cargo of spelter in the Hornby Dock (the northern dock) and, as the wind was from the north-west we had to tack the vessel down the river against the wind. I was at the helm when we left the dock, with all sails set to beat down, tacking from one side of the river to the other. As soon as we left the dock, my uncle came aft and said to me, 'All right, Hugh, I will take her now!'

But I was determined that from this time on I would be in sole charge. Right or wrong I told my uncle, I was quite capable of taking the vessel myself, and I gave him an order to clear up the decks. 'What was the matter with me' he asked, 'had I ever docked in the Hornby Dock?'

I told him, 'No,' and that I would dock the vessel that day without anyone's help.

It was not long before we were in a position to make for the dock entrance. I kept the vessel before the wind and being empty and with a fresh wind blowing, she travelled fast through the water. I told my uncle to lower the foresail to check the vessel's way, but he answered. 'No! keep it on her. You will need all the way you can get to enter the dock head to wind.'

'Do as you are told' I called back in reply, 'and lower the sail.' This he did but when I brought the vessel head to wind I found we had barely enough way to enter the dock. After we had managed to get a rope ashore the Dock Master said to me, 'Captain, you should have kept your foresail on a little longer.' He was right, I knew.

When we had loaded the spelter cargo we left the dock bound for the berth at John Summer's steel works above Connah's Quay, so we had to navigate the rock channel. My uncle seemed to be little offended by my refusal of his help, and as he was sure I was not acquainted with this channel asked me to let him have the helm. He explained that he knew it well. 'No' I replied, 'I can manage quite alright, thank you, and there is plenty for you to do about the deck.' As a result of this, when we arrived at Connah's Quay, he gave me notice and left.

I was now without a mate and it was not easy to get anyone to accept the berth in a little craft like mine. I had taken on my cousin as cook and it was his first ship. We were loaded with fireclay goods for Douglas and at last I managed to persuade a man I knew to make the round trip there and back with me, this man's intention being to go salmon fishing when he got back.

We were leaving Connah's Quay and I had brought my clothes from home in a canvas bag. I was standing on the quay and threw my bag, as I thought, on the deck, but it fell short between the ship and the quay. Someone managed to save it and haul it on board but there were several old sailors standing close by who witnessed what had happened, and one of them remarked, it was a bad omen. He recalled a similar happening and told how after the vessel sailed, she was never heard of again. I took no notice of what he said but my new mate, who was afraid of the sea and very superstitious, was impressed by what he heard.

The same day we towed to Wildroads. The barometer was falling and a fresh south wind was blowing accompanied by drizzling rain. When the tug boat let go the towropes we set all sail and started the trip. After getting clear of the sandbanks at the mouth of the Dee I set a course for Douglas Head and set the log. We ran on until we had almost run our distance by this. Visibility was poor and as I could not make out the light on Douglas Head we reefed the mainsail, hauled in the sheets and lay to. There was very little movement in the sea and we were quite comfortable. I went below for a few minutes; then my cousin came down and told me the mate was in a panic. I went on deck and found him in a real fright. He asked me should we get into Douglas that night and when I said that we should not, he moaned, 'Oh dear! it is quite right what the sailor said when your bag fell in the water. We shall never be heard of again.' I ordered him below and told him to turn in.

A few hours later the weather cleared and we could make Langness Light and Douglas Head. Soon we were in Douglas harbour. We returned empty from there to Connah's Quay and the mate signed off, only too thankful to get off the ship just as fast as he could.

I was now again without a mate and my vessel was once more loaded and ready to sail. I was at home when there came a knock on the door, and my mother on opening it came back to tell me that there was an awful looking man asking for the berth as mate, adding that she hoped I would not ship him. I went to the door and there was a strange looking man with a full white beard, tobacco stained around the mouth. He wore a pair of dungaree trousers, a number of tattered cardigans and over all this a couple of pilot jackets. I could just see the top of his blue shirt and all together he looked as if he was in need of a wash. 'Have you been mate of any vessel before?' I asked him.

'If I was not fit for the berth I should not have applied for it,' he replied. As I thought he would be better than no one, I engaged him and told him that if he had nowhere to go he could go aboard that day. However, when I went aboard next day, he was there all right. My cousin, who had remained on board, thought the old man a queer old stick. We towed to Wildroads the same day and as the weather was too unsettled to sail, we anchored there. As the mate was, I thought, an experienced sailor, I went home leaving him in charge of the *Elizabeth Hyam*. Within a few days with a change in the weather I returned and we sailed for Belfast. The old man still wore all the same clothes and my cousin told me he was sure the old man had not washed himself since he came aboard. He added that he had hardly spoken a word to him since he joined the vessel.

The weather was the same as on my previous trip to Douglas, and our course was to the Chicken Rock on the south end of the island. After passing the Chicken lighthouse, the ship's course had to be altered. I stayed on deck until we had passed to the south of the island. The wind had veered to the west and we had good visibility. I gave the mate the course to steer, north north west, which was close hauled, and I went below to have a few hours sleep. Before long I was sure, by the vessel's movement, that she was off course. The wind was strong and it seemed to me we were going with the wind abaft the beam. I went on deck, to find the vessel was heading north

north east. I asked the mate why he was steering that course and he replied that it was the course I had given him. As I could not trust him to steer I told him to go below and turn in. I then remained on deck until we dropped anchor in Belfast Lough. This was on a Saturday, the following day we towed to Belfast.

On Monday morning, at a quarter to six, I called the mate, as work began at six a.m. and continued until six p.m. He came on deck in the same slovenly dress and it was evident that he had no intention of washing himself, so I told him if he was going to remain on my ship he would have to keep himself clean. He was extremely indignant and told me I was the first person who had ever said he was dirty. We were loaded with 'quarries' and the crew had to help discharge the cargo, the mate having to stand on deck and catch each twelve inch tile from the man standing on a stage in the hold. Then he had to throw it to the man standing on the quay. He had also to count each tile as it passed through his hands. When a hundred tiles were counted, he put a stroke on a tile, and when five hundred tiles were counted he would put a stroke through four strokes with a fifth one. Working this way, a considerable number of tons would pass through a man's hands in one day, and leathers had to be worn to protect the hands from the tiles. I could see it was hopeless to expect the mate to do this work at his age, although it was his duty to do so. I took his place on deck and I told him to prepare the meals.

'No,' he said, 'I shipped here as a mate, not as a boy, and I refuse to do boy's work.' I could do nothing with him and so we had to make do with scrap meals prepared by myself.

When the cargo was discharged, we hauled the vessel to the dock gates and at high water we were ready to return to Connah's Quay to load for Ireland again. Arriving at the gates the mate informed me that he could not sail, claiming he had broken his foot. 'Broken your foot?' I asked. 'How and when?'

'It is enough for you to know I have broken my foot,' he said. By now I was firmly convinced that he was taking advantage of the fact that I was not very old. Ever since he had come aboard he had been a nuisance.

I hauled the vessel back and tied up alongside a little schooner. When the vessel was moored I demanded to be shown the injured foot. 'No,' he said, 'I will not show you my foot, you are not a doctor. I will go to hospital. You have no sympathy with an old man but you will be old yourself one day.'

The crew of the schooner, alongside of which we were lying, were leaning on their bulwarks listening and watching what was going on, and they appeared to be in sympathy with the old man. One of them told me I should be ashamed of myself. When the old man realised he had their sympathy, with great and apparent difficulty, he climbed over the vessel's rail on to the quay, calling back in a pitiable voice that he was going to hospital.

Then he started to walk towards the main street, dragging his leg and appearing to be in great pain. He had to turn a corner to get to the main street, and he went on, dragging his foot, walking very slowly until he reached the corner. Then he looked back to make sure no one was following him, and disappeared. The crew of the schooner had watched him go out of sight. 'Now!' I said to them 'Come with me and see if he is still dragging his leg now no one is watching him.' We all jumped ashore and ran to the corner. The old man was walking quite easily, with no sign of a limp....

The old man was back aboard before long and no longer pretending that his foot hurt, but I had by this time determined to have no more of his nonsense, and I told him that if he did not behave himself and go about his work in a proper manner I should pay him off. I then went to the Sailors' Home and shipped a superior young man as mate and we both came back to the vessel. The old man was still there and he accused me of being hard hearted, casting an old man adrift in a strange country, with very little money. I offered to let him make the trip back with us. 'Yes, and work for you for nothing?' was his reply. At last he went. I have never met anyone like him before or since.

We sailed with the new mate who had never been in such a small craft before. The little *Elizabeth Hyam* rolled and tossed about so much on this trip that, unaccustomed to this kind of vessel, he asked to be paid off when we arrived. He had very little in wages to draw, so I paid his fare back to Belfast.

The young man Tom Jones who had been shipmate with me on the *Hilda* then came mate with me, and a very happy time we had together. One event happened which I remember well. We loaded a cargo of dressed granite at the little port of Annalong in County Down for Barrow-in-Furness. As we were entering the latter port, the breeze died away, and as the vessel was drifting out of the channel with a strong flood tide, I dropped the anchor to check our drift. The tide was running at about four miles an hour. The anchor brought the vessel up, and with the way the tide gave her I was able to get the vessel into the channel, the bottom of which was hard, with the result that the chain parted and the anchor was lost.

We anchored in Piel Roads for the night, and on the next high water we arrived in the long dock, at the entrance to Barrow Dock. The Dock Master, noticing we had only one anchor, asked me what had happened. I explained to him how and where our other anchor was lost. Barrow Dock comprises a large expanse of water, making it necessary to employ a tug boat to reach the discharging berth. We hauled from the dock to a berth to await the tug.

Next morning, the mate and I were sitting in the cabin, when a messenger hailed the vessel to say the Head Harbour Master wished to see me at the Harbour Office, at once. So far, I had had very little experience as Master, and of the liabilities for which my vessel could be held responsible. A little knowledge would have saved me a lot of anxiety at this time.

Arriving at the office, I was shown into a comfortably furnished room where a shorthand writer was in attendance with the Harbour Master. The latter began questioning me, adopting the attitude of a cross-examining counsel and speaking with an amazingly superior accent; 'You lost an anchor last night, Captain?'

'Yes, that is right,' I said.

'Where?' he inquired.

'In the entrance to the Channel off Haws Point,' I replied.

He spread al arge chart of the port on the table. 'Do you know anything of a chart? If you do, point out to me your exact position where this anchor was lost.'

I pointed out the position for him on the chart, every word I said being taken down in shorthand. He then asked me what steps I proposed to take to recover the anchor. As the spot where I had lost it was several miles from the dock and exposed to the sea, I was amazed at his question. I replied that I had no intention of making any effort to recover it owing to the difficulties involved.

'You haven't?' he said, 'Well, the sooner you change your mind, the better it will be both for you and your owners, that is, if you have any regard for your owners. I suggest that you take my advice and get in touch with a local fisherman and arrange with him to leave on the next morning's tide. Take a grapnel with you and when you reach the place where you lost your anchor, drag over the position until you recover it.'

This suggestion left me speechless and he went on to dismiss me, saying, 'That is all I have to say to you, for the moment. Do as I advise and it will be very much to you and your owners' interest.'

I left the office feeling depressed. It was going to be a difficult matter to find a fisherman who would undertake this job, and how much would it cost to engage a boat for twelve hours? When I told my mate the bad news he was as concerned as I was, but we both agreed that it would be advisable to do what the Harbour Master had suggested.

We went ashore and found a fisherman, and having agreed on the charge, it was settled that my mate and I should accompany the fisherman in his boat, leaving the dock at four the following morning.

We set off as arranged. It was a cold, rainy morning, and the weather did not improve during the day. We dragged the grapnel all day long but all we discovered were large stones on the bottom, much larger than our two-hundredweight anchor. By the time the next high water came, we were tired, wet and hungry, and when we eventually docked I went straight to the Harbour Master to report the failure of our effort.

'Oh well!' he said. 'I will put the harbour tug at your disposal and I will instruct the master to be in attendance for the morning's tide. You will accompany him and instruct him where he should commence to drag the grapnels and you will continue until you recover your anchor.'

I looked at the Harbour Master in amazement. I do not know when I have disliked a man so much. I told him I had no objection to going with his tug but it must be clearly understood there would be no liability on the part of my owners for expenses.

'Oh indeed!' he said. 'Well you please yourself whether or not you accompany the tug. I suppose you do not realise what the liability would be on your owners if a steamer entering the port should be holed, by striking your anchor.' I told him there were stones on the bottom much larger than my anchor, and I failed to see what liability could be on my vessel for a ship striking the bottom.

'I can see you do not appreciate that I am trying to help you,' he replied. 'If you will be guided by me, you will go with the tug on the next tide. You will also pay for the tug's services before your vessel will be allowed to leave this port.'

I boarded the tug the next morning and we proceeded to where the anchor had been lost. The two grapnels were dropped overboard over the stern and the tug's speed set at slow. We had about ten hours steaming ahead; unless of course the anchor was hooked sooner. I sat on the engine room casing, and began to think I had acted like a fool to have taken notice of what the Harbour Master had advised. I also realised that I should have asked my agent's advice before doing anything.

The captain of the tug came and sat beside me, asking what was the trouble between me and the Harbour Master. I told him the whole story. He thought I was very foolish to have taken any notice of his orders. The day passed with no results and we docked again. By now I was feeling more angry with myself than with the Harbour Master and when I reported to him the failure of our efforts, I told him I was no longer interested whether the anchor was recovered or not, and that I was doing nothing further in the matter. 'Well,' he replied, 'if you will settle the tug's account, I will give you your pass to sail and we will consider the matter settled.' My answer to this was that I had gone with the tug under protest and I would not pay for its services.

I then went to my agent, Mr. Fisher, to whom I told the whole story. He told me I should have asked either his or my owners' advice before agreeing to anything the Harbour Master had to say. I told my agent of the threat to withhold my pass to sail, unless the tug's account was first settled. On hearing this, Mr. Fisher sent a messenger to the Harbour Office demanding the pass to be given unconditionally and immediately. It was given without question.

I was now gaining experience fast and I soon had occasion to learn more when we were in Liverpool and I was seeking a cargo. Sometimes no cargoes would be offering but there was always the hope that a good freight would one day be offered for somewhere. On this occasion, my agent offered me a good freight for a cargo of coal to a small place in Anglesey, called Cemlyn. It did not occur to me to enquire if Cemlyn was a safe port to fix for, I just took it for granted.

When we arrived, the wind was from a southerly direction, a smooth water wind blowing off the shore. I took the vessel into Cemlyn Bay and came to anchor. Then I looked around for a place where we could lie to discharge the cargo. To the west, in a corner of the Bay, I could see the lifeboat house, with a steep slipway, to the right of which was a steep shelving beach. A cottage was close to the lifeboat house in which the coxswain lived. I went ashore in our small boat and called on him.

Not unnaturally, I was very concerned that nothing should go wrong with my vessel, for my owners were running her without any insurance and if anything should happen on my first command it was very doubtful if I would ever be offered another. Furthermore, it was now the month of December and I believed I had done a fine piece of business to charter for this place.

I asked the coxswain where we had to discharge and he pointed to the beach. I was of the opinion that if the wind shifted to the north while the vessel was there she would be broken up. He agreed with me. I told him I supposed the cargo would be discharged in one day but he thought three days at least. Hearing this, I felt that I must see the consignee and impress upon him the need to hurry the discharge. The coxswain told me the merchant lived several miles away and he pointed out to me the direction, saying there was no proper road and that I could easily lose my way. Nevertheless, I set out.

I walked some distance and eventually came to a farmhouse. I knocked on the door and my knock was answered by a girl of about sixteen years old. I enquired was the master in, but she did not seem to understand my question. She motioned me to enter and I followed her into a large room that was filled with people. There were men, women and lots of children as well as servants. The merchant's wife came forward to greet me but she knew no English and what little Welsh I knew was useless to carry on a conversation. The children hid behind their mother's skirts and peeped at me as if I were some strange thing. Then tea was served and I joined in around a big table. At last the merchant arrived. He was a happy jolly man and seemed glad to see me. He asked if I had had a good trip and would I join him in his meal. They seemed an exceptionally happy family but I was too anxious about my vessel to enjoy any conversation with him or to join him at his meal. I wanted to know when he would commence the discharge and how long it would take. He advised me not to be too anxious and assured me that nothing would be gained by it; that three or four days should see the cargo unloaded. By now it was getting dark and time for me to make my way back to my ship. The merchant sent his son part of the way with me, until I was sure I could find the way myself.

At high water, I put the *Elizabeth Hyam* on the beach and as there was nothing I could do to hasten things, I could see it was useless to worry. The wind was off shore and with luck would probably remain so. As it was, it turned out we were lucky, for after three days our vessel was empty, there was no shift of wind and we sailed out of Cemlyn, heading home for Christmas.

CHAPTER VI

My schooner J.C.R. *— I become captain of the* Sarah Latham *— loss of the* J.C.R. *— the* Lady Fielding *at Abersoch — a collision with the trawler* Lucerne *— the irate owner*

MY AGENT IN CONNAH'S QUAY ALWAYS SPENT HIS holidays in the Isle of Man. On returning from one holiday there, he informed me there was a nice little schooner in Castletown, called the *J.C.R.* which was for sale. He asked me why didn't I buy her, as it was a fine opportunity for me to start shipowning. I was not really interested as I was doing very nicely with the *Elizabeth Hyam*, but my agent never missed a chance of telling me that I was foolish not to make an offer for her, and continually urged me to go to Castletown to inspect her. Finally I sent my brother Tom to inspect her and to give me his opinion of her qualities.

His report was that the *J.C.R.* was a grand little craft and I made an offer for her which was duly accepted. I sent my younger brother William with the cheque to get the bill of sale, to complete the purchase and bring the vessel home in readiness to start trading.

My first sight of my new acquisition was when I was passing through the Menai Straits bound for Caernarvon, early on a fine summer morning off Beaumaris. There I saw an old vessel at anchor, which seemed to have been laid up for years. I thought, surely this is not the vessel I have bought, but it was indeed. The *J.C.R.* looked a wreck to me. I came to anchor, went aboard her and wakened my brother. He was still of the opinion that I had a great bargain but I believed that whatever the vessel was, or had been, I had not sufficient cash to pay for the reconditioning necessary before she was fit to trade. I looked over the vessel with dismay and I knew I had only myself to blame, as I should have inspected the vessel personally.

It took three months to complete the repairs which were absolutely necessary for her to go to sea and really she needed a lot more. I did not insure her, which was another unsatisfactory way to start shipowning. My brother William remained as her master with my brother Tom as his mate, but I still regretted my purchase.

When the *J.C.R.* started trading I myself had a new command, the *Sarah Latham*. She had been built to carry sheet iron from Messrs. Summers' works at Shotton near Connah's Quay to Liverpool and Birkenhead for shipment abroad. She was quite modern, of shallow draft with large hatchways, but her bulwarks were very low, making her unsuitable for general coasting. Almost as soon as she was built, the contract for carrying the sheet iron was given to the railway and the *Sarah Latham*, together with a number of other craft, was deprived of a profitable trade. Her master refused to go coasting in her, leaving her owner at his wits' end to know what to do with this new vessel which had cost so much to build.

A friend of the owner offered to sail her and so she loaded a cargo of fire-clay goods for Belfast. Arriving there, the owner chartered her to load at Dublin for Connah's Quay, but when the vessel arrived back in the Dee, her new master refused to make another trip, saying she was not suitable for the general coasting trade. I was interested in this vessel and hoped I should be offered the berth of master, for I considered she was a much superior vessel to the one I was in. Several captains told me they had been offered the berth and had all turned it down, but when the owner did not succeed in finding a captain, he approached my agent to know if I would accept. I was not too pleased at the manner in which my agent passed on the offer to me, for he gave me to understand that if I approached the owner through him I was almost certain to be appointed master.

'Well', I said, 'if he wants me to be master of his vessel, why can he not ask me direct?'

'That is nonsense', my agent replied, 'What difference does it make? All you have to do is accept the offer and you secure the berth.'

'No', I said. 'You can tell him to come himself and ask me, then I might accept.'

Two days passed by and the owner did not come and I had become quite indifferent about the whole affair. Then, the owner and his son came alongside my vessel and asked could they have a word with me. When I stepped on the quay, the owner said, 'Your agent tells me you are agreeable to take charge of the *Sarah Latham*'. My reply was that the agent had no authority to give him that information. 'I had only informed him that if you wished me to take charge of your vessel you would have to offer me the berth yourself.'

'Then,' he said, 'I am offering you the berth myself.'

'And I accept,' I replied.

I took command of the *Sarah Latham* shortly afterwards and was very pleased with my new vessel. My agent offered me a cargo of coal for Abersoch from Garston, and he assured me that, although this had to be discharged on the beach after the tide had ebbed out, it was quite a safe place. No vessel had come to harm there, he went on to say, but my owner was not at all pleased when I informed him that I had chartered for Abersoch. He told me the insurance did not cover any damage that could happen to the vessel while we were there for it was one of the ports barred.

At about the same time that I loaded the Abersoch cargo at Garston, my brother William loaded a cargo of slates in my schooner the *J.C.R.* at Portmadoc for Waterford. When I arrived at Abersoch, the first news I received was that the *J.C.R.* had been wrecked on the Splock Rock as she was entering Rosslare Harbour, where she was making for shelter. The crew were safe but the vessel was a total wreck. As there was no insurance on my vessel I lost all my savings—though it was a great consolation that no lives were lost.

Abersoch, on the Lleyn peninsula, was a port where spring tides were necessary for a vessel of any size to enter and we had only a day or two to spare when we arrived. The merchant told me he had another vessel chartered for this port which had been loaded quite a time before us, but he was afraid that the morrow's tide would be the last for her to enter before the next spring tides.

The following morning, the vessel he had spoken of, the *Lady Fielding* arrived, and she rode to anchor off the port. The weather had turned stormy and there was every sign of a severe gale blowing up. I was concerned at her arrival, as there was not too much room on the beach for two vessels to lie abreast. They would have to be securely moored with ground moorings to make sure they did not come together.

It was nearing high water and the *Lady Fielding*, rising and falling to the big swell that was coming in, showed no signs of getting under way. Even though it was not too good to have the vessel in with mine, I thought it was hard lines for her to stay in the roads for a week in this kind of weather; so, I pulled off to her in our small boat and asked her captain why he was not under way. He replied that he was waiting for a pilot. I told him there was no pilot, but if he was agreeable, he could rely on me to take his vessel in and to this he agreed.

We had no trouble getting in and made the *Lady Fielding* fast to wait until low water, when we could lay out ground moorings. I was at great pains to point out to her captain how important it was that his starboard anchor should be well off, and backed by a second anchor to make sure it did not drag. I was sure the anchor they carried was much too light to hold any strain, and I offered the loan of a heavy stream anchor to back his but he would not accept my offer. He was of the opinion that his anchor was sufficient to hold his vessel. I was very worried, because if my vessel should be damaged without any insurance cover it would be a serious matter.

There was no doubt we were in for a bad night and there was no mistake about the gale, which reached its height as darkness came on. By high water, when both the schooners had floated, a big swell was coming in, causing them to range about wildly and putting sudden strains on the moorings.

At last, what I was afraid of began to happen, the *Lady Fielding*'s anchor began to drag. With every range the schooners came closer together, until the *Lady Fielding* smashed into us. With the first crash, the whole of her port bulwarks were stove in, others followed and the two vessels continued to collide and pound each other until the time the tide had ebbed. The *Lady Fielding* was then so badly damaged she became a total loss. Being a very old vessel her damage was regarded as irreparable, while my vessel, new and strongly built of oak, hardly bore a scar.

Our cargo of coal now discharged, it was necessary to secure another one. Captains would often spend considerable sums of money in telegrams and telephone calls enquiring what cargoes were offering. At this time, as no cargoes were offering, I decided we should move to Holyhead, as I had been informed that crushed stone was being shipped from there to Liverpool.

We got under way from Abersoch and into St. Tudwal's Roads.

The wind had shifted to south south east, a fair wind to get around Bardsey Island. After passing through St. Tudwal's Sound, we opened up the light on the Island, which as we were heading, was well away on our starboard bow. The *Sarah Latham* was going through the water at a good rate and with the wind in the direction that it was and six hours ebb tide under the lee, I was in no doubt we would pass Bardsey before the tide turned.

After a couple of hours however, the wind died down and it started to rain; then the wind began to freshen from the south west. My vessel, being empty, was making no headway in the short choppy sea and with the wind getting up, I realised I was in a situation of great danger not only to the ship but also to my crew. This is a very dangerous shore to be embayed upon yet there was nothing we could do. It was no use tacking ship for that would only make matters worse. Our only hope, and a faint one, was that we would drift through Bardsey Sound. I watched the Bardsey Light show more on the port bow, and then become obscured behind the Island, and then, after a very anxious time, appear again to the east of the Island. We had drifted through the Sound and so were out of danger. Thankfully we squared away for the South Stack.

Arriving at Holyhead I sought out the agents, or shipbrokers, to see if they could charter us for a cargo of stone. In every port where ships trade, there is an agent. Some ports have several and the first thing a master does on arrival is to seek an agent, give him the ship's papers and the agent then does all the ship's business for an agreed fee. If he arranges a charter, he charges five per cent on the estimated freight; he also advances cash for wages, and finally, just before the ship sails, he presents all accounts which are settled by the master.

The agent I found in Holyhead enquired of me what carrying capacity the *Sarah Latham* had, the size of her hatchways and the draught of water. He asked where I had discharged my last cargo and what freight I had been paid. When I told him the amount, he remarked, 'My word! that is a lot of money to receive for one cargo. You have a good vessel and if you like to put yourself in my hands I can make your fortune. I can fix you for plenty of cargoes.' I replied jokingly that I had been hoping for a long time to meet someone who could do just that.

He then contacted the manager of a local quarry who agreed to load us. But now my agent asked me if I would first load a cargo of coal at the Point of Ayr Colliery. I agreed, the charter was made out and we sailed for the Point of Ayr at the mouth of the Dee. While we loaded there, I went home to settle accounts with the owner and to bank some money, as I was anxious to save after the loss of my own vessel off Rosslare. I returned to my vessel and paid the crew their wages.

We arrived back at Holyhead with the coal cargo on a Saturday, after being away for only four days. In the evening, the crew who were going ashore asked me for a sub. I had not expected them to ask so soon after being paid their wages, and I was in consequence rather short of money. However, I knew I would be sure of collecting the coal freight on the following Tuesday.

'All right', I said, 'one of you come with me. We will go to the agent, and I will get a couple of pounds from him and you can have it between you.'

The agent did not seem very pleased to see me, and when I asked him for two pounds, which was quite a usual practice, he said, 'What do you want two pounds for? What have you done with all the money you had the other day?' I felt so angry with his offensive manner that I replied. 'You don't call that a lot of money do you? It only lasted me a couple of days, I drank it.' As a matter of fact I was a strict teetotaler.

It was a relief to be out in the street again, and I decided that when I had loaded the cargo of stone I would find someone else other than this agent to help me make my fortune.

But it was difficult to find work trading short, so rather than lie idle, I chartered to load fish-curing salt in Ramsey the Manx port for Buncrana in Lough Swilly. This is considered a difficult trip for a small vessel but we were fortunate and made the trip without delay.

It was the herring fishing season in Lough Swilly, and I never before saw so many drifters in one place. I was told there were four hundred and fifty vessels fishing out of the port while we were there. There were drifters from the East Coast ports of England and also from Scotland. The herrings were gutted by Scots girls, then salted and put into barrels for export. The price paid for them was very small. I bought a cran for four shillings and sixpence and good size cod-fish for a penny each. I was given some home-made Scotch oat-cake by one of the fishermen and it tasted good. The cod-fish and ling were caught while the boats were lying at their nets, by means of what the fishermen called a jigger, which was a piece of lead about ten inches long with three cod hooks on each piece. The fishermen would jig up and down all day long and they caught a lot of fish this way.

Buncrana was a very busy port and while we were there we loaded bog ore for Ellesmere Port, at two and ninepence a ton, the ship to pay the cost of discharge.

Our next cargo was bone ash for Gatehouse-of-Fleet, a small port on the north side of the Solway Firth. Leaving the dock, we groped our way in foggy conditions clear of the Mersey. The fog got worse, with only a light air from the south, just giving us steerage way through the water. We gave the usual fog signals at intervals through the night. The next day, a steam trawler suddenly loomed out of the fog, and, striking us a glancing blow on our starboard bow, went across our path knocking away our bowsprit. He then disappeared into the fog. Before long he was back, groping his way by the sound of our fog horn. The trawler, we found, was the *Lucerne*, of Fleetwood, and her skipper enquired if we were all right and did I want a tow in. As the damage was not serious I assured him we could manage to make our trip and thanked him for his offer.

It was difficult to fix our position, as we were not going through the water fast enough for the log to register. We took casts of the lead every so often and the following morning at seven a.m. I took a cast and got ten fathoms. We lost no time in letting go the anchor. After the vessel had come head to into what little wind there was, I took from the stern another cast of the lead and got a shock. We were lucky to be afloat. At about nine a.m. still surrounded by fog, I heard a steamer's whistle, the sound coming from the south of us. We saw nothing; then at about eleven o'clock the fog began to lift and from our stern I could see the lapping of the water, white against the rocks, only a few yards away. It was a sheer stroke of luck that we had got the anchor down when we did. As the fog cleared away, we noticed a ship's boat pulling towards us, with four men aboard. They made fast alongside us and said they were the crew of the steamer whose whistle I had heard. Only that morning they had left the little port of Whithorn and shortly after I had heard their whistle, their ship had struck rocks and sunk.

The land under our stern was the island of Fleet in Wigtown Bay, about six miles from Gatehouse-of-Fleet and we reached the quay there that evening. Eventually we did a lot of trading with the south Scottish ports and I became familiar with most of them.

The following January, when we were in Runcorn, as no other cargoes were offering, I loaded a cargo of fertiliser for discharge at several places in Milford Haven. At this time my brother William was with me as mate. My owner thought it was foolish of me to do this trip at that time of year.

However, we made a good trip and discharged our cargo, and as no other cargo was available, I loaded anthracite at the Hook, Haverfordwest. This was for Penzance, where we arrived during the night after making a good passage. Next morning, I went ashore to see my agent and in the street, I met two Connah's Quay captains, whose vessels were also in Penzance. They were Captain Richard Conway and Captain John Manifold. I mention this incident to show what poor opinions the local captains had of my vessel's sea-going qualities. When my friends saw me they asked, in feigned surprise. 'What has brought you here? Has the *Sarah Latham* sunk and have you been picked up by a steamer and landed at Penzance?' I was delighted to be able to tell them that my vessel was at the Albert Pier and ready to discharge a cargo of coal. 'If that is so,' said Captain Manifold, 'then you deserve the V.C.'

Within a few days we left for Runcorn with a cargo of china-clay. Soon after leaving, a severe south west gale sprang up, before which we ran for twenty-four anxious hours. The *Sarah Latham* was not the kind of vessel to heave to, deeply loaded as she was and with such low bulwarks. A steamer, believing we were in danger, kept close to us all one day, and we must have appeared to her captain and crew like a halftide rock.

But we arrived safely off the Mersey and towed to Runcorn with the fine three-masted schooner *M. E. Johnson*. She had also been in the gale. After we had moored alongside, her captain told me of the big seas that were running and how he had had to lay his vessel to. We were together on her deck while he told me this, and looking down on my vessel, low in the water and with her low bulwarks, I

Captain Hugh Shaw

*His father,
Captain Humphrey Shaw*

A rare photograph of Connah's Quay, showing the wharves alongside the Dee, in the 1880's. [Photo: Flintshire Record Office]

The Quay House at Connah's Quay where Captain Hugh Shaw was born.

jokingly said; 'Now, if you had been in a fine vessel like mine, you would have had no anxiety!' 'Aboard your vessel' he replied, 'had you been where we were last Wednesday, she would not have lasted one hour.' 'Nonsense!' I remarked, 'we were running up the same time as yourself and we did not find it necessary to heave to.' To convince him I had to take off a hatch cover and show him our cargo of Cornish china clay.

It was always better to sail under a long established owner, whose experience gave him an understanding of the need for caution in sailing these coasters. If a captain got impatient and lost gear and sails, he got no thanks from his owner even if he did make his passage, for in the owner's opinion, it was no use earning a freight if it had to be paid away to repair loss of sails. I should like to tell what happened to a captain I knew who sailed under a man who was the owner of his ship, but who knew nothing of shipowning.

This man was a coal merchant living in southern Ireland and he bought an old schooner cheap. He bought her in September, engaged a captain and chartered her to load coal from Garston, consigned to himself in southern Ireland. The captain, who was my friend, did the trip in record time and brought the vessel back empty to Garston for a second cargo. By the time she was loaded with the second cargo the weather, which had been very fine, changed to stormy and unsettled, and the captain, who was a good coaster, knew it was imprudent to sail. A week passed by with no improvement in the weather and the owner, getting impatient, sent a telegram to the captain to know if he was still in dock. Thinking the telegram too foolish to warrant an answer, the captain did not reply. A second telegram arrived and was ignored until finally the owner himself came aboard, seeking an explanation. He peremptorily ordered the captain to get his vessel to the dock gates and sail.

Southerly winds blow down the Mersey as far as the Crosby lightship, then the course alters. The captain, under the orders of her owner who had stayed aboard, sailed the old vessel at good speed past the Rock lighthouse, with a strong south south west wind. Passing the Crosby, they had to haul into the wind, and when they came to the Bar lightship they were faced with a moderate south west gale, a confused sea and a heavy mist. The old vessel was shipping water and labouring, and as for the impatient owner, he was seasick. He ordered the captain to take the vessel back to anchor, but this could not be done until the flood tide made, and it was highwater when at last she came to anchor in New Ferry, with everyone tired out after a day's unnecessary frustration. After the sails were furled and the captain and owner had had a meal, the captain could not resist the temptation to tease the owner by suggesting to him, that as he (the owner) was such a successful businessman, he may like to tell him how to do his job. The owner replied that he did not wish to discuss the matter and remarked that it would not worry him if only one cargo a month was discharged. 'One cargo a month!' replied the captain, 'you will never have one cargo a month in this old ship.' 'Then,' said the irate owner, 'I will cut the masts out of her.' To which the captain replied, that he had better get his axes sharpened!

CHAPTER VII

Discharging cargoes – have you paid your 'income tax'? – voyages to the Solway Firth – to Preston off the Bar Buoy – Arlingham on Severn – a meeting

WORK AT THIS TIME WAS NONE TOO PLENTIFUL, AND we had to charter for any cargo that was offered. With most of these, the ship had to pay for the cost of discharging. I recall loading a cargo of light cast-iron scrap in Dublin for Lancaster, but when I saw the class of scrap, it worried me as to how I could discharge it economically, for it consisted of such items as old broken saucepans and thin pieces of metal which I was afraid would take most of the freight to pay to discharge it.

When I arrived at Lancaster, the quay was crowded with men, with at least twenty there seeking work. They asked did I require men to discharge my cargo. I enquired what they charged, and they informed me their charge was one penny farthing per ton. I engaged seven men and each man received just fifteen shillings and sevenpence halfpenny for three days of hard work, in helping to discharge one hundred and fifty tons of scrap.

On another occasion, I loaded a cargo of crushed granite in Carlingford for Manchester and the cost of this discharge was sevenpence per ton. I employed five men, with the use of a crane and its driver. The whole cost for the day's work was £4. 7. 6d. About this time, in May 1909, while I was still in the *Sarah Latham*, we arrived at Garston with a cargo of timber and came to anchor in the channel, between Dingle Point and the Dock. I was surprised to see quite a fleet of coasting schooners lying there in the channel and so I made enquiries from the captain of the one nearest to us as to why so many were there. He told me that all were bound for the dock but some had been in the channel for weeks. He himself had lain there for over a week and had no idea when he would dock. 'Well!' I thought, 'this is just too bad!' Outside the loss of earnings by the delay, constant watch had to be kept for vessels passing through the narrow channel leading to the dock.

All vessels had to be booked in at the Dock Master's Office, before being allowed to dock. I was feeling pretty miserable when I entered the office and I asked the gateman, who handed me the book to sign, when he thought we might enter. In what sounded more like a snarl, he replied. 'When the other craft have docked will be time enough for you to ask that question.' Making my way back, I was passing a vessel loaded with timber whose captain I knew. 'Hello!' I said, 'how long is it since you arrived?' 'Oh! he replied, 'only a couple of days ago.' 'Well' I said, 'how is it you are in dock and all the others are out in the channel.' 'Ah' he replied, 'they have not yet paid their income tax.' I asked him to explain.

'If you want to dock on the next tide', he said, 'go back to the booking office, and tip the gateman; you will dock all right.'

Back to the office I went and put a half-crown on the desk in front of the gateman. 'When will we dock?' 'After the others!' was his curt reply. I put another half-crown with the first one and continued to add more, until there were six on his desk. Then he said, 'You can bring your vessel to the dock gates'. We docked without any questions being asked.

I am going to describe two trips which clearly illustrate the risks run by small coasters, which were my trade and my life. On the first such trip, I loaded a cargo of maize in Belfast for Dalbeattie in Kirkcudbright, during a period of stormy weather. When I left Belfast Lough the wind had shifted to the north east—ideal for a vessel bound for the south Scottish ports, making a weather shore and smooth water. After passing the Mull of Galloway, the wind died down to a calm but a big swell was coming up from the south west. The sun was almost obscured and the barometer was falling rapidly. All the vessel was doing was rolling about, with no wind to go anywhere. It would be high water at about mid-day in the port to which we were bound and if we missed that tide it would not be possible to enter at midnight, as there were no leading lights.

The southerly gale I was expecting, started before daylight, and having the wind, we had ample time to reach our port by high water, providing visibility was good enough to make our headlands. This was the beginning of a severe gale and by the time I made the last headland it was blowing a full gale right on the shore, with blinding rain and a big sea running. We had to make Heston Island at the mouth of the estuary up to Dalbeattie and there we could make shelter. The compass was all I had to rely upon, with visibility down to much less than a mile.

I remembered from a previous voyage there were a number of fishermen's stakes that could be seen at high water and to see them would prove there could be no mistake about the Island.

We were almost on the Island when I made it. There were the stakes all right and I left them on the port side, steering for the village of Kippford, which later came into view. I had been in this port only once before and I knew that the channel runs close to the shore and that I needed a pilot. Several men, who had been watching our vessel entering on such a bad day, were sheltering behind a wall from the wind and the rain. As I got near to them I hailed them to ask where the pilot was. They yelled back to me to let go the anchor while we were yet safe. We did so and the *Sarah Latham* came head to wind and tide after a tricky few hours. Later the pilot came aboard and put the vessel into a safe berth.

The second trip was from Dalbeattie to Preston with a cargo of crushed granite. We set sail, and when the pilot left me, he took with him a telegram to the Harbour Master at Preston, advising him that I would be off the Bar Buoy on the next morning tide, and to have the pilot and a tug in attendance. High water would be some time after seven a.m. There was a fair wind and we arrived in the Ribble estuary in good time, but no tug or pilot hailed us. The tide passed, the wind now freshening and blowing right into the estuary. I was not feeling very happy, for a new channel had been opened, and I had no sheet of the port and my old chart showed nothing of the channel. As neither the tug nor the pilot had attended the morning's tide, it was doubtful if they would attend the next one, so I decided I must find a safe anchorage somewhere.

A steamer which had left Preston on that high water hailed me with a message from the Harbour Master to say the tug had been out on the morning tide, but had mistaken my vessel for a trawler. My orders now were to cruise off the Bar Buoy and the tug plus a pilot would be out to me without fail at five-thirty that evening.

It was a long wait, with a strong wind and every appearance of a gale. As the afternoon wore on, it was necessary to carry as much sail as possible, to hold our own off the buoy, and with our heavy cargo of granite, the vessel was making very bad weather of it.

The time of year was December and it was dark at five-thirty. At that hour the buoy was away to windward of us and we were losing ground. My crew wanted to know if I intended to let the vessel founder, or was I going to run to leeward and safety. As I had no idea what course to steer to find the channel, I refused to run to leeward.

As darkness set in I began to give up hope of the tug coming and it was almost six p.m. when at last we made out some navigational lights. It was the tugboat. He came under our lee and hailed us through a megaphone to say he would endeavour to put a pilot aboard. I thought this an unnecessary risk as I could follow the tugboat into smooth water but they put a boat out and the pilot got into it by himself and crouched low down in the bottom of the boat. The tugboat went ahead towing it. The waves were so high, that one minute the little boat would be halfway up the rigging of our schooner and the next minute out of sight below the ship's rail. At last, watching his opportunity, the pilot jumped from his boat on to our deck. He certainly was a brave man. I thought, as he jumped, that he would injure himself, but he was not hurt and he scrambled up, calling out as he did so 'Hard up! Skipper, Hard up!' He came close to me at the helm and we were soon running before the gale. 'Have you a good tow rope, Captain?' he asked, 'for as soon as we reach smooth water we will get the tow-rope on to the tug. We have eighteen miles to go and only two hours to do it in.' This was secured: no light task and indeed it was no easy task even to steer behind the tug at the speed she was going. These Preston boats were big and powerful and my vessel was small, but we docked safely.

Whilst we were in Garston I met a Gloucester captain. He was Captain Henry Aldridge, whose vessel was moored alongside mine. After we had completed loading, I sailed, and we did not meet again until the following September when we were both loading cargoes in southern Ireland for the Bristol Channel, he for Bristol and I for Newport. He gave me an invitation to visit him at his home at Arlingham, that is if we should both arrive at the same time.

We did, and he met me at Newnham railway station. Newnham stands on the opposite side of the river from Arlingham and the ferry on the river is about a mile from the station. Waiting in the ferry boat to take us to the Arlingham shore was the grand old ferryman, Tom Phillips, or 'Old Tom' as he was affectionately called by everyone. I got to know him well later on, and became very fond of him.

The village of Arlingham was a mile from the river crossing, and arriving on foot there, in very fine weather, I thought what a lovely little place it was and how I should like to live there.

I received a great welcome from Captain Aldridge's wife, and after tea we went into an orchard where I helped to pick fruit, which was in abundance, especially Victoria plums. Later in the evening we visited the Captain's parents. There was no difficulty in finding something to talk about, of course it was the sea and ships. I just could not get over my amazement at finding seafarers living in this farming community, so far from the sea.

The next morning, I decided I must get back to my vessel. Captain Aldridge, who became Harry to me, pressed me to stay another day, and so we both agreed that we would cross over to Newnham to phone my agent, to find out if my vessel would load that day. He informed me that we should not load until the next day, and that being so we returned to Arlingham.

I spent most of the afternoon helping to pick fruit, and then at about tea time, Harry's young sister came into the orchard. She had just returned from a holiday and had brought presents for her brother's children, and watching her with the children as she talked to them of all she had seen on holiday, I thought whoever marries her will be a very lucky man indeed.

After we had been introduced, we went to her home and had tea with her people. We stayed with them for the rest of the evening, it being late when we returned to Harry's home. I went to bed, but I found it impossible to sleep, my mind being in a whirl, thinking of this charming young woman. 'I must see her again,' I told myself, 'what excuse can I think of to come to this place again?' After going over these problems for an hour or so I came at last to a decision. In the morning I would call at her home to say goodbye to her parents and I would ask her to accompany me on the mile walk to the ferry.

Next morning I carried out my plan. At first she hesitated when I asked her to come with me, but when I asked her a second time she agreed to accompany me. It was a lovely September morning when we set off together. I was very happy walking beside her, and we talked quite a lot; but what we talked about I have no idea, for my mind was busy trying to think how I could ask if I could see her again.

We were at the ferry in no time. Old Tom was there and I had said nothing. At last, just as I was getting into the boat I said to her, 'I have never met anyone I like so much as you. If I write you a letter, will you answer it?' She made no reply. I got into the boat quite certain she must have thought I was slightly deranged. Old Tom chatted as he always did as he pulled the boat across the river but I did not hear a word he said.

When I got aboard, my vessel was loaded and we sailed. I was impatient to get to our destination. I wanted to write her a letter and I was even more impatient to get an answer. As soon as we reached Newport, I wrote telling her how much I had enjoyed my visit and if I were permitted, how I should like to come again.

To my joy she replied, saying, her brother would be pleased to welcome me, any time I cared to come. I was delighted to receive a reply and I wrote to ask her if she would like me to visit them again. To this letter I had a reply from her saying it would be nice if I could spend Christmas with them.

We sailed next to my home port, Connah's Quay. It was no good thinking that I could wait until Christmas to see her, for I simply could not wait that long. So I wrote to her to say I was coming to spend the next weekend with them. My mother was curious to know why I was not going to spend my weekend at home, asking me where I was going and who I was going to see? I do not remember ever going anywhere before from home. I told her I was going to see my future wife.

On the train I did not think much about anything and it was only when I came to the ferry and saw Old Tom's face, all smiles, and remembering how he had watched me when I said goodbye to her only a short time ago, that I realised my secret was not my own. But I need not have worried about Old Tom, who was incapable of poking fun at anyone; he had far too kind a nature for that. However, I began to wonder as I got out of the boat and started to walk to the village, if the people I had come to see might think it strange and be amused at my swift return, especially as I had invited myself.

If that was so, then I saw no sign of it when they greeted me, and they made me most welcome.

During my stay, someone asked me if I had ever seen the Severn Bore, assuring me that it was worth seeing, and so we set off on our second walk together. It was delightful to walk with her again, there was no embarrassment and there was no effort to talk, we might have known each other for years.

We talked of the sea and of the long separation it caused between husband and wife, as well as of the anxieties and disappointments of being a sailor's wife. Belonging to a sea-faring family, coping with these conditions came naturally to her.

We forgot about the Severn Bore as we wandered on, and it was only when we heard the roar of the tide that we remembered it. After a few more visits we became engaged, and as there was no reason for us to wait, we were married at Arlingham church. This was on January 19th 1910. From then on, we never lost the thrill of meeting each other after our unavoidable separations or the joy of being together with our five children. It was great good fortune for both of us to be together for forty-one happy years.

I like Arlingham, where I have spent so many happy years; the people who live here are my good friends and neighbours. Among my good friends are the local coasting captains. To mention two who sailed from the port of Gloucester; Captain Bill James, whose family owned the beautiful little *Elizabeth Drew* and Captain Sam Watkins of the family who owned the lovely schooners *Despatch* and *Earl Cairns*.

CHAPTER VIII

Part owner of Kate, *of Barrow, 1911 – windbound at Holyhead – a gale at Christmastime – loss of the* Harvest Queen *– a cargo to Cardigan*

I MADE MY HOME IN ARLINGHAM, THE VILLAGE WHERE MY wife was born, and I am still as fond of this place as I was on my first visit, the happiest days of my life having been spent here.

In 1911, my father-in-law, Captain Lewis Aldridge, and I bought the schooner *Kate*, of Barrow. We bought her cheap as she was quite old but she was a good sea-boat. I left the *Sarah Latham* and took charge of the vessel of which I was now half owner.

It was by no means easy to make these old vessels pay. Winters were the trouble, stormy weather causing the vessels to lie windbound for long periods. To try and force them very often resulted in the sort of hardship and loss that happened on a trip we made in 1912 from the Mersey to Bridgwater.

After leaving the Mersey, we had to seek shelter in Holyhead, the weather continuing stormy until near to Christmastime. Over sixty vessels were sheltering there with us, including several belonging to my home port of Connah's Quay. Some of the captains proposed, as the weather was so unsettled, to moor their vessels safely and spend Christmas at home with their families. When they asked me was I coming with them, I replied, it was too long a journey to Gloucester. Instead they urged me to spend Christmas with my parents. But I did not go, for I was anxious to make the trip, and on the Sunday evening before Christmas, December 22nd, the strong southwesterly wind eased up. There was not any prospect of making much progress, for in tacking against this contrary wind, four miles would have to be covered to gain one mile to windward. But I suppose everyone was anxious to make a start and one by one the various schooners and other vessels got under way and left the harbour. We left with them and getting clear of the breakwater, found the breeze much fresher.

We went through the water quite fast and fetched Wicklow Head on the first tack; we stayed and fetched the Bardsey; tacked ship and we were heading to fetch somewhere north of the Tuskar. We fetched in to windward of the South Arklow lightship at midnight of the 23rd. We had the whole of the ebb in our favour and I was hoping to make the anchorage of the south bay by low water.

I took the wheel at midnight; a severe gale was now blowing with bad visibility. It soon became evident that we could no longer struggle against the wind and the sea and we ran back for Holyhead. We were under small canvas and I kept the *Kate* away before the wind. The mainsail gybed, and although the sail was rolled up small, the main boom broke, making the mainsail useless. The gale blew with even greater violence. All the sail we had set was just the peak of the boom foresail.

We made the South Stack light at 5.30 p.m. I had been at the wheel since midnight and all the crew had remained on deck, there being too much water about the deck to think of food. It was useless to try and enter the harbour as we had no mainsail and it was necessary to beat in from the breakwater to get to the anchorage: even with a well-found ship this would be a difficult operation. We had no option therefore but to carry on, past the Skerries, past Point Lynas, and to seek shelter in Wildroads. We came to anchor there at four o'clock on Christmas morning, minus bulwarks, and with torn sails which would take months of trading to pay for. Our water tank was full of salt water and the beef cask had gone over the side together with everything moveable about the deck. Anyway, we were still alive. Exhausted, we turned in and had a good sleep.

The following morning we put our small boat out and got a supply of fresh water from one of the other schooners lying to anchor. As the wind had eased, I decided to go to Flint and see my parents. I landed on the bank at about 4.30 p.m. and walked to Mostyn railway station. I had one hour to wait for the train which ran a Sunday service. The station was only dimly lit and the waiting room had no fire. It looked a most desolate place and the rough time I had had helped to add to the gloom. I stood on the bridge that crossed the railway line and I looked out at the few lights, shining in the darkness, of the schooners lying to anchor in the roads including those of the *Kate*. I thought of the words of the man who told me I would have more kicks than ha'pence if I went to sea . . . .

By the time I arrived at Flint I was feeling much better. I walked into my home and my parents and my young sister were delighted to see me. My father remarked that it would have been better had I come sooner, believing that I had left my vessel in Holyhead. When I told him my vessel was in Wildroads, he said, 'Then you have received a lot of damage. You should have known better than to be caught in such a severe gale.'

Yet we came out of the storm better than some. The schooner *Harvest Queen*, a better ship than ours, was lost with all hands, and several others were in more trouble than we were, on different parts of the coast. But we had had a bad trip and two of my crew deserted; they did not intend to have another like it.

It was quite a time before things were in order and we could continue trading, but during the next two years we did quite well, enjoying long spells of favourable weather and successful trading. Two voyages at this time are worth mentioning. In January 1914 we loaded dressed granite in Penryn for the port of Erith. I think the smallest stone weighed more than five tons. On the day we completed loading, a gale from the south-west gave us a very anxious night, a heavy run came in the harbour, causing the vessel to range at her moorings and kick the bottom. We managed to haul off the buoy in the middle of the harbour, and somehow managed to hold the vessel by taking in the slack when the vessel ranged, and to stand by and ease the ropes when the strain came on. It was a great relief to see the tide ebb out and leave us dry on the bottom.

After discharging the granite at Erith we loaded a cargo of fertilizer for the port of Cardigan, at what was then considered a big freight, 12s. 6d. per ton. The reason the extra freight was paid was because there was considerable risk in entering Cardigan, which had a shallow and rather difficult channel. Arriving off Wales, we lay in Fishguard for a few days to await the tides. During this time I arranged with a local steamer to tow us in and this ensured, we arrived safely.

CHAPTER IX

Outbreak of World War I – my father joins as Mate – cargoes to Ireland – Youghal – Clonakilty – coal to France – a dangerous trade – the Kindly Light *– the* Katie Cluett *– the little pilot – the Armistice*

WE WERE SHELTERING IN HOLYHEAD WHEN, A FEW months later, World War I was declared. Two of my crew who were Naval Reservists had to obey the call up, making it necessary for me to find two fresh sailors. Several vessels in Holyhead with us at the time had their whole crews taken. We carried on quite well until November 1914, when I was left with no crew and little hope of getting one. My father, now retired and past seventy years old, offered to come with me until I could get another mate, and I gladly accepted his offer.

I chartered for a cargo of coal from Newport for Youghal, thinking as I did so that I might be lucky and ship a couple of sailors in this Welsh port. A few seamen were there looking for a berth and I made arrangements for two of them to join me, but after seeing the class and size of vessel which they had agreed to join, they failed to turn up next day.

We now had the cargo aboard and would have to deliver it. The weather was good with a moderate easterly wind. I proposed to my father that we sail, just the two of us, but he was doubtful and wondered how we would manage the topsails. Anyway we left Newport and stayed the night in Cardiff Roads. Next morning, the wind still being fair, I went aloft and loosed the topsails. We hove up the anchor, set the sails and in fact we had a good trip without any hardship or troubles.

After arriving in Youghal, I was lucky to ship an A.B. who was reputed to be a good sailor, and I would like to say here that the seamen of Youghal are known to be very fine sailors. I had been hoping to have shipped a further man here, but was not able to do so as almost all belonged to the Naval Reserve and the few that were left were crews in local vessels.

By the time we had discharged and loaded a cargo of oats for Bristol it was near to Christmas. We had had a long spell of southerly winds which were contrary for making our passage. Several schooners owned in Youghal were lying with us and had been waiting for weeks for a shift in the wind to make their passages. One morning, going on deck, I found a change. The wind had veered to the north west giving promise of a fair voyage and home for Christmas. My A.B. came aboard but he had a sad event to tell, for his father had died in the night. He would be staying at home until after the funeral. I expressed my sympathy to him and we agreed that if I sailed before the funeral he would remain at Youghal over Christmas and then join me after the holidays, and I would advise him where to rejoin.

I felt very disappointed at not being able to take advantage of this favourable wind, and having decided that it was blowing too strong to attempt the trip with only my father on board I went ashore. As soon as I stepped ashore I was met by some of the captains of the Youghal-owned vessels who had been windbound for so long, and it being so near to Christmas they did not welcome the prospect of leaving home: if I did not sail, they had a good excuse to give their owners for not sailing. They asked me was I sailing, and I replied, 'No, how can I? My A.B.'s father had died and so he will not be able to sail with me until after the funeral.' With that they went home to dinner, thankful they would not be sailing that day.

Highwater was at 4.00 p.m. The tide had swung the *Kate* and the freshening wind right aft was blowing her against the tide ahead of the anchor. I became restless with that fine wind blowing away and suggested to my father that we heave in some anchor chain. 'What good will heaving in the anchor chain do?' he replied.

But we manned the windlass. When the fifteen fathom shackle came in sight, the flue of the anchor was there with a turn of the anchor chain around it. A foul anchor.

The crews of the local vessels always had their midday meal ashore at their own homes and I saw that two of the vessels' boats were now returning. I hailed their crews and offered a gratuity if they would clear the anchor, and they came to my assistance. I told my father to go to the wheel and keep the *Kate* straight until we had the anchor clear. Soon we had it clear and catted. The men also helped me get the ship's boat secure on the hatch. I went aloft and loosed the topsails and the Irishmen helped us hoist and sheet them home. We set the boom foresail and the jib, and were now forging ahead against the tide in fine style. I paid my helpers and they had to scramble into their own boat in a hurry, we were sailing so fast.

I went aft and took the wheel from my father, who laughed and said, 'Well! you beat the band!' 'It is all right,' I said, 'I will steer her all the way and with this wind it will be quite easy.'

There was no need to set the mainsail. The wind was dead aft and there was rather a big sea. We were doing quite a bit of rolling but we were getting along through the water at a good speed.

At 8.00 p.m. I asked my father to go below and turn in. Exactly twelve hours later at eight the next morning we passed the St. Govan's lightvessel; there was now a fine fresh wind still blowing dead aft. My father brought me a cup of tea and took the wheel while I went below and had my breakfast. I returned and took the vessel, advising my father to go below, there being no use in his standing on deck for hours.

We came to anchor at 2.00 a.m. the following morning in Kingsroad. It was still blowing hard and it took a lot of chain to hold the vessel, which would mean a tough job ahead for two men to heave it in again. We both turned in and it seemed no time at all when a voice called out, 'Skipper! are you down there? Where are you bound?'

'To Bristol,' I replied.

'Well,' came back the voice, 'we are the Bristol tug. Hurry up! Shall I call your crew?'

'I have no crew,' I replied.

It was a dark cold morning and there was the heavy work of heaving in the chain, so I offered a sum of money to the captain of the tug to share with his crew, to heave up the anchor and clear away our tow rope. They were willing and with the tugboat alongside to take the strain off the anchor chain, we were soon away and so up the Avon to Bristol.

Later, I heard that I had offended my friends, the captains of the Youghal schooners: after being assured by me that I would not sail, they went home. At low water their owner walked down to the quay and, noticing that my *Kate* was no longer there, inquired of a fisherman when we had sailed. He told him I had sailed that day— and with only one man. The owner was furious, for his ships were much finer and larger vessels than mine and carried six men. He routed out his captains and made them sail the next day, which unfortunately proved a day too late, for after they had left the wind backed to the southward and they had to seek shelter in Passage East. There they spent their Christmas!

The 'sink on sight' campaign of the German submarines began about this time and the losses to our class of vessel were very heavy. The Admiralty gave each ship routing instructions, but with a sailing vessel it was not always possible to carry them out. At times we were compelled to make our passages in the best way that we could, and very often, as in my own case more than once, by not carrying out their routing instructions we made a safer passage.

Because of the submarine sinkings, the losses of the mutual insurance club, by whom we were covered, were so great that heavy calls were made upon us, and it would take us all our time to earn enough money to pay them. Eventually, the club went into voluntary liquidation and from then on we were able to insure at more favourable terms.

Most merchants in Ireland who imported the coal carried in our class of vessel were also grain merchants, and exported grain to England. To make sure of obtaining a craft to carry their grain, they had a clause inserted in the coal charter whereby the master must give the consignee the option of the vessel for the outward cargo. This clause was worded 'To all ports in the English and Bristol Channels.' As the submarine risk became greater, the difficulty in securing tonnage for any of the English Channel ports increased, and to make matters worse, although the grain fetched higher prices, captains refused to give merchants the option for these ports.

I had been running for some time for one merchant in Southern Ireland to the Bristol Channel ports, and when I went to sign the Bills of Lading, I was more than surprised to see that the port of destination for my cargo was Plymouth. I said to the merchant, 'You knew perfectly well that you had no authority to consign my vessel to an English Channel port, so I refuse to take the cargo. The only option I gave you was for the Bristol Channel ports.'

This merchant was, I think, just about the most determined and stubborn man in the whole of Ireland. Once he had made up his mind to a course of action, nothing would shake him. I thought that

A painting of the two-masted schooner Kindly Light, *sunk by a submarine in the first World War.*

The schooner Camborne, *for many years owned and skippered by Captain Shaw.*

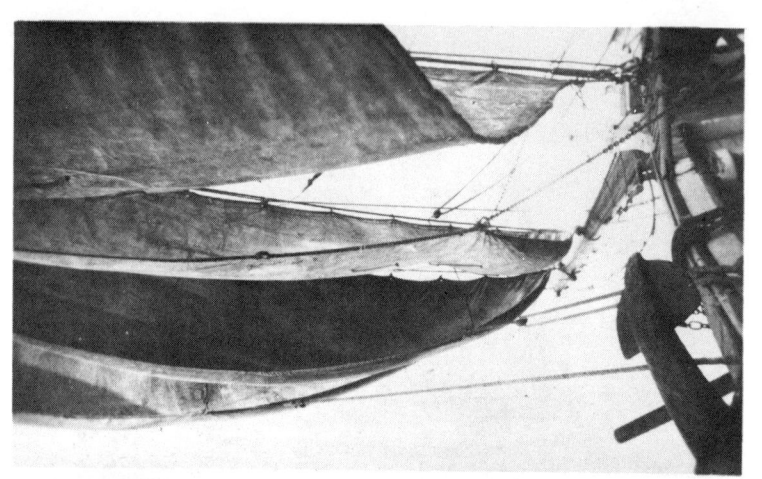

On board the Camborne.

rather than waste time standing out for my rights, I would take the cargo and thereafter finish trading with him. It was more than three years before I did business with him again.

I next traded with a merchant in Kinsale until early in 1917. By this date nearly all the sailing vessels trading to the ports of northern France were being sunk by enemy submarines, and the demand for tonnage was so urgent and the risks so great, that shippers were offering in one freight more than the value of such a vessel. I was quite unaware of the big freights that were being offered. I had just discharged a cargo of coal in Kinsale at 19s. 6d. per ton and the merchant wanted me to charter again at the same rate. I asked 20s. The day was Saturday and as the merchant would not agree, the matter was left over until Monday. On Monday morning I received a letter from a colliery agent in Newport (Monmouthshire) offering me £4-10-0d. per ton on a cargo of coal from there to Fecamp, with half the freight to be paid in advance. I could hardly believe what I read. I wrote in reply giving him authority to charter my vessel for the best terms he could secure.

Arriving at Newport, we had a cargo of pit props to discharge. The coal agent was at the dock entrance and I asked him had he chartered me at £4-10-0d:

'No', he said, 'I have fixed you at six pounds per ton and you can draw half the freight before you start.'

My wife was distressed when she heard that I had chartered for such a dangerous trip, but I explained that the risks were not all that much greater than in trading to Ireland. Sailors' wives are used to their menfolk taking risks and everyone at this time was taking risks of one sort or another.

We loaded, and our instructions were to make our way the best we could to Falmouth, and there we would join a convoy and be escorted across the Channel. I was fortunate to arrive in Falmouth just in time to join a convoy, as sometimes there would be a long wait until there were enough vessels assembled to form one.

We were only escorted as far as Cape Barfleur; from there onwards we were on our own. We had a light westerly wind and the weather was fine but hazy, with visibility down to about a mile. Several times French patrol boats hailed us, enquiring our destination and advising us to keep nearer to the shore, for U-boats were in the vicinity. But despite this advice, with visibility so poor, I thought it wiser to keep to a straight course.

The next morning we made out the white chalk cliffs at Yport, close to Fecamp, but it was hard to distinguish the land clearly, and the dark water marks running down the white chalk looked at first like the masts of a ship. The haze cleared a little and when we got close to the entrance to Fecamp, a tug came out between the piers and came alongside us. The pilot came aboard. 'Take the tug Captain,' he said, 'there are plenty of submarines about.'

I duly took his advice and we were soon safely in the dock. I was elated at making the trip so rapidly and both the pilot and the tug captain could see I was in a good humour. They lost no time in taking advantage of it.

'You give me twelve miles pilotage, Captain?' the pilot said.

The tug captain also asking to be paid for twelve miles towage. I agreed, but found that in doing so I had doubled my expenses. It was much the same with the customs men, whilst the dock gatemen demanded a gratuity before they would open the dock gates.

We loaded flints in Fecamp for Cardiff and I also chartered to load at the latter port for St. Brieuc. When we sailed the naval authorities ordered us to proceed from Fecamp to Caeux to join convoy. I decided that as there was a fresh south-west wind blowing and as it was also getting dark, I would risk the crossing without an escort. I soon discovered that I was running even greater risks than from any submarines, for we ran into the track of numerous transports. They were taking troops and stores to France and travelling at great speeds in the darkness, without showing navigation lights. It was a great relief to me to reach the English shore at daylight and we beat down channel as far as Brixham where we anchored. When the wind came fair we left there and continued our voyage. Soon after we passed Land's End, quite a few schooners there were sunk by gunfire from a U-boat. Several men were killed getting their boats out, the commander of the submarine giving the crews no time to clear from their ships before opening fire. On the same day, a friend of mine, Captain Watkins, had his schooner the *Kindly Light* sunk by a U-boat only a few miles ahead of us.

We arrived at Cardiff and loaded the cargo for St. Brieuc. We made the return to Falmouth without incident and were fortunate in catching a convoy again. Our instructions from the naval base were to pass to the east of the Douvres Rock as we entered St. Brieuc Bay, and not attempt the Barnac channel as it was mined. The escort went ahead and we were in the rear of the convoy which consisted of about twenty sailing coasters.

We had pretty well run our distance by the log, and according to my compass the course we were steering was too far to the south to pick up the Douvres Rock light. I considered it prudent to lay too, until the weather cleared, and after lying too for four hours, I picked up the Douvres Rock light and passed it, leaving the light on our starboard beam. Meanwhile the whole convoy, with their escort, sailed on without us. Later on, when we had docked, I talked with some of the other captains who had been in the convoy. One told me, that after they had sailed on without me, he was down below when his mate called out, 'Skipper! There is a white light almost abeam.'

By the time he reached the deck, the white light had turned to red, and soon was showing white again. This was the lighthouse on Brehat Island and the red light showed the danger sector over the Barnac Rocks. The whole convoy had sailed through the mined channel like sheep going through a hedge, but without loss. I told them they would live longer if they sailed their own ships and not followed someone else's.

Much the same thing happened on our trip back to Cardiff. The weather was misty with bad visibility, and the whole convoy was almost ashore before they knew where they were. The fine schooner *Katie Cluett* ran ashore on the Dodman and her captain was drowned. Before this, after dark, I had left the convoy and steered the *Kate* for the Scillies, and then around the Longships safely and so back to Cardiff.

We continued to trade to St. Brieuc or to Paimpol without incident but we often had long waits in Falmouth harbour for an escort. From these French ports, the rendezvous for the return convoy was at Lizardrieux. On one occasion I left St. Brieuc and entered Paimpol harbour. From here there was a channel through the rocks to Lizardrieux. I had been through this channel once before with a pilot. I came to anchor close to where the pilot lived and I pulled ashore in the ship's boat to go to his house. There I saw the pilot's wife and son, a boy of about twelve. Neither could speak English, but in my indifferent French I made her understand that I needed a pilot. She told me her husband was away and would not be home that day. I wondered what to do, for although I was fairly sure that I could navigate this channel, I was afraid of the danger that I might put the vessel ashore.

The boy was watching me. The boys of French pilots go with their fathers at an early age and they know all these intricate channels like knowing a street.

I said to the pilot's wife, 'The garcon, he bon pilot?'

'Oui! Oui!' they both replied.

The little chap came aboard with me and we got under way. My young pilot stood by the rail, watching the progress of the *Kate* and not speaking until I asked him if all was well. I would say, 'Bon? Pilot?'

'C'est bon, Capitan,' he would reply.

We caught the convoy. My little pilot had earned his pilotage.

On another occasion we had a long wait for an escort. There were enough ships for a convoy but the weather was stormy and escorting vessels were not available. Every day, all the captains of the English vessels would go to the naval base to demand an escort, or at least permission to sail without one. The commander grew tired of our demands, as he had no power to order an escort for us or allow us to sail without one, but I suppose we felt we had eased our feelings in asking. At length, two armed trawlers put in an appearance to escort us over, and the Commander in his launch visited every vessel to order them to get under way.

The barometer was falling and there was every appearance of a gale; not the sort of day to leave harbour with vessels in ballast. I hailed the nearest vessel to us, a ketch, to ask her captain what he intended to do. He thought exactly as I did. We both decided not to sail until there was some improvement in the weather. The Commander was angry at our refusal to obey his orders, and the trawlers sailed on without us.

That night a very severe gale blew right on the shore. It would have been disastrous had we sailed, and as it was, two vessels dragged their anchors and were wrecked on the rocks close to us in the harbour. A French vessel dragged past us in the height of the gale, doing considerable damage to our bulwarks until he dragged clear.

After a few days, the gale blew itself out, and we now returned to the Commander, who gave us a very cool reception. He said it was useless for him to provide an escort if we refused to sail when one was provided. I was appointed spokesman, and I explained to him how difficult it would have been to beat out clear of the outlying rocks with vessels in ballast, to which he replied, 'Then none of you know the harbour. There is no need to beat out clear of the outer rocks, for there is a channel inside the rocks leading to the sea.' Spreading a fine sheet of the harbour in front of us, he pointed out this channel. It started from the outer end, close to a small round island, little more than a rock, on which was a red painted tower. This rock was called 'La Roche Rouge'.

After several days more, another escort turned up. It was late in the afternoon before we started on our course, and it took quite a time to get all the craft together outside the port; by that time, the wind was freshening and shifting more to the north, with the sea getting up. Under these conditions, none of the vessels were making any progress, and at last the signal went up from the escorting destroyer 'Return to anchor as convenient.'

That was some order, more easily issued than carried out. It would soon be dark and this was one of the most confusing of ports to a stranger. I noticed two French schooners heading away for 'La Roche Rouge'. Good, I thought, these are local men, making for the short cut channel, which the Commander showed us.

It was blowing quite fresh and the *Kate* was going through the water fast. I looked for the leading lights but they were too far away to make out. We followed the two schooners making for the channel and soon overtook one of them. When the leading schooner was abreast of the Red Rock, we were close under his stern. Their crew were watching me, but did not hail or make any sign. My guide, after passing the rock, hauled into the wind, his sails taking the wind out of mine and enabling me to keep close to him without overtaking. After passing the rock, I saw at some distance ahead, a black perch, well away on our starboard side. The vessel ahead suddenly luffed, until he brought the perch on his port. Why he did this, I soon found out when he went to starboard. I did the same, and then close under my lee was a dark patch of water. There could be no mistake. It was a submerged rock with very little water over it: we had only missed it by a few feet. After passing this, the Frenchman brought the perch back on his starboard, which was a relief. Watching the second schooner coming up astern, I was concerned to see that he was not making any effort to clear the dark patch, and he sailed right on to the rock, and there he remained. I followed my guide until I reached the anchorage and with great relief let go our anchor. Two other vessels returning to their anchorage became total wrecks on this occasion, and a friend of mine struck a rock, just managing to get his vessel in before she sank.

On getting back to the Bristol Channel, we were in Swansea when the D.A.M.S. (Defensively Armed Merchant Ships) officer came aboard, and informed me they were going to put a six-pounder gun on the deck of the *Kate*. We would also have to accommodate two naval gunners. Two masted schooners were awkward craft on which to fit a gun but this was duly fitted, just halfway between the mainmast and aft, right in the centre of the deck. It could only be fired at about 45 degrees on each side, on account of the masts and the rigging, and when the officer asked me what I thought about being defensively armed with a six-pounder, I told him it struck me as a good idea of suicide.

I was sure that my two gunners had never fired a gun in their lives. They were salmon fishermen from Southern Ireland, and had joined the naval reserve for the sake of drawing the retainer. These poor old gunners would cheerfully have refunded all they had received to be back salmon fishing again.

We left Swansea with a fair wind bound for Morlaix. This carried us as far as Trevose Head, when the wind came to the west—a fine sailing breeze. We had been advised by the naval authorities only to sail when the wind was fair and to hug the shore. Despite this I thought, 'a few tacks to windward and we will be around the Longships'; so we remained at sea.

A few hours later we were standing in to Cape Cornwall on the starboard tack not far from Land's End. I had just finished my midday meal and had taken the wheel. I was watching two steamers who were close under my lee, expecting them to pass around our stern. Suddenly a column of water shot up from the bow of the leading steamer. She had been torpedoed and began to sink by the head. We were so close I had to tack ship to avoid colliding with her. The steamer sank rapidly but the crew were safe in their boats. I tacked ship to go towards them but my help was not required, for the other steamer took them aboard and steamed towards the shore. I then stood off on the port tack. There was no sign of any U-boat and I could see no sense in the watch below remaining on deck, so I told them to go below, which they did.

About two hours after the watch had gone below, right ahead of us I saw a U-boat surface. I watched its bow and conning tower come out of the water and I shouted to the gunner who was in my watch to get his mate on deck and man the gun. I had to keep the vessel away, to get broadside on to the U-boat in order to enable our gun to bear. In this position the *Kate* was broadside to the swell and rolling heavily. I thought, 'I have managed to escape a good many awkward experiences but I am afraid this is one too many for me.'

I told the gunner to get the gun trained on the submarine but when he had it all ready to fire, he said that he was not allowed to attack, only to fire in defence. He tried to sight through the telescopic sight but it was impossible to do so for the *Kate* was rolling too much. Then a strange thing happened: the U-boat submerged and that was the last we saw of her.

We arrived safely in Morlaix and discharged but we had to wait a long time in Morlaix Roads for an escort. Only a few vessels were there. The naval authorities wanted us to go to Lizardrieux for convoy, but the others were not willing, so there we remained. While we were waiting, we ran short of bread and I had to go to the town of Morlaix to obtain some. I had to stand in a queue with a crowd of French women waiting to be served, and they, discovering that I was English, became most unfriendly and demanded to know what right I had to take their bread away from them. It was fortunate for me, that at that moment, a French Board of Trade surveyor who knew me, was passing by, and seeing me standing in the midst of these hostile gesticulating women, came to me and took me to another baker, giving him orders to supply me with what bread I required. I was grateful to him for this, but what bad bread it was. Black and sour! The food in France was much worse than it was in England.

Our next cargo was for Paimpol. This was a great shipbuilding port, where a lot of the Grand Bank fishing schooners were built. Whilst we were there, one of my gunners went for a walk in the country. He was dressed in his naval uniform and on his walk met a German prisoner-of-war who was working on a farm. The latter asked him in good English, 'How is the war going on, Jack?' The gunner replied, with a smile, 'Oh! we are pushing you back a bit now.' Which was true, and a few days later the armistice was signed and the war was over. The whole town went wild with joy. The French had suffered dreadful losses and hardships and it seemed to them the news was almost too good to be true.

After the armistice was signed, no one was very interested in doing any business, for a time. Our vessels had discharged their cargoes but we could get no satisfaction about our freights. There were several English vessels in the port, and our agent advised us to go to the consignee's office in St. Brieuc and collect our freights. We made the journey by train and were having a cup of coffee in the station restaurant, when several American sailors entered. Thinking we were Frenchmen, one of them said, in what he thought was good French, 'I expect vous beaucoup pleased la guerre est fini.' We all smiled and one of my captain friends replied—speaking for all of us—'Not half, mate.'

CHAPTER X

Trading to France with coal and pit props – profitable charters – the Mary Miller – at Portmadoc – an engine for Kate

WE CONTINUED IN THE FRENCH TRADE, WITH COAL OUT and usually loading cargoes of pit props from different ports back to the Bristol Channel. Some schooners, however, loaded potatoes for Spain. New freights were fixed at a much lower rate but there were plenty of cargoes to any port we cared to charter, for tonnage was scarce.

At this time, several coasting vessels were being fitted with auxiliary engines, and I was determined to fit one in mine. The *Kate* also needed a major re-fit. I found a shipbuilder in Portmadoc who would undertake the work of repairs on her, plus the installation of an auxiliary, and having decided on what engine I would install, I arranged to have the whole work done. This was to be after I had made one more trip, to St. Brieuc.

We made the trip after a stormy passage but I was in excellent spirits, due to the thought that I should soon have an auxiliary in my vessel, which would be such a great help in trading. With this advantage, we would be able to get along in calms and would also be able to enter harbours without the aid of a tug.

The morning we commenced discharging our cargo at St. Brieuc, the manager of the firm receiving it, who incidentally was an Englishman, called on me to enquire if I would be interested in chartering for a further number of cargoes of coal, from Cardiff to St. Brieuc, combined with return cargoes of pitwood. I told him I was not interested, because I intended to have an auxiliary engine fitted and also to have the vessel re-conditioned. This information did not deter him, for he asked me how long it would take before the ship would be ready to trade again. This I estimated would be about three to four months. 'Will you charter with me when your ship is ready?' he asked. 'I can offer you twelve cargoes of coal, to return with pitwood at 52s. 6d. per ton, and 14s. per ton on the timber loading, with discharging free.'

I asked him could he charter under those conditions immediately, and he replied, 'No, not immediately, I must first pass this on to my head office in England for confirmation, but first, can I have your offer so that I can write?' I said that he could.

Now I felt that I must have a talk with my agent, so I went to him and told him of the offer. He asked why had I not given another merchant, for whom I had carried many cargoes, the opportunity to fix my vessel. 'Surely,' I replied, 'is it not a little mad to be chartering so far ahead, and at such a high rate?'

'No captain, it is not,' he said, 'for we need twenty million tons of coal in France. You say you have signed nothing yet, so I will send for the other merchant, you may get better terms with him.'

The merchant was sent for and was soon in the office, very excited. 'Captain,' he said to me, 'I treat you good. Every time you load for me I give you good offer, Yes! Then why you not charter with me to carry my cargoes?'

I appealed to my agent to explain my position, and the merchant having understood said, 'That is all right. I will charter you now, for the same number of cargoes, at three pounds per ton.' I accepted. Now I asked my agent to contact my English friend, the manager, which he did by telephone. I took the 'phone and spoke to him. 'Have you written to your head office in England for confirmation of the charter?' I asked.

'No,' he replied, 'it is not an hour yet since I spoke to you.'

'Well,' I said, 'unless you are prepared to accept my offer now, do not write.'

'All right,' he replied, 'have it your own way but I cannot accept until I get authority.'

The charter was made out, and I made sure as I thought that there would be no clause that could break the charter. The merchant was as anxious as I that there would be no loophole and he asked me would I sign an extra document to the effect that should the government requisition my vessel I would still complete the contract. I felt I was certain of very profitable years of work ahead.

Two days later a messenger came from my agent, asking me to attend his office. There my agent introduced me to a man, who said he wished to buy my vessel. What was my price? Things were moving just a bit too fast for me to think clearly. I asked the agent about the charter I had signed two days ago. 'That is why this gentleman is anxious to buy', he replied, 'he will take over the contract.'

'Well,' I said, 'I will not sell under two thousand five hundred pounds.' My father-in-law and I had paid four hundred and fifty pounds for the vessel in 1911 but I knew what had happened to prices in the meantime. The man answered immediately that he would give it.

I asked the buyer to give me until next day, when I would give him a considered answer. I had had what I thought was a good idea. Messrs. Fisher, the well-known owners in Barrow, had a lovely three-masted schooner called the *Mary Miller* which I had always admired. She was in excellent condition I knew, and a fast sailer. I decided I would send a cablegram to Messrs. Fisher and offer them four thousand pounds for her, subject to an immediate reply.

But the reply I had from them said they were not disposed to sell at the moment. I thought, 'Fishers are experienced ship owners and if they refuse an offer like this, then I had better hold on to my vessel,' so I did not sell.

So, from St. Brieuc, we proceeded to Portmadoc to install the engine in the *Kate* and we arrived at the end of January 1920. This was the beginning of a period of frustration, worry and unnecessary expense. I expected the reconditioning to begin more or less as soon as we arrived, but all the carpenters were engaged on work on the schooner *David Morris* which was passing her survey there, and it was several weeks before work could be started on my vessel. When work at last commenced, the weather set in wet and stormy, and the carpenters could not work, there being no shelter. So the weeks dragged on.

My wife and two of my boys came to Portmadoc to keep me company. They all had been looking forward with pleasure to staying in North Wales, but were disappointed to find that all they could do, day after day, was to stay indoors, in the most dismal of lodgings, with rain falling incessantly.

Everything we required for the *Kate* was difficult to obtain, and repairs to her were exceedingly slow. It took weeks to bore through the stern post for the shaft to go through. My wife, the children and I went home at last to the comfort of our own house. Then just as the work on the ship was completed, the government stopped the export of coal to the Continent, because of the impending threat of a national coal strike. As a result my charter was cancelled. The boom in shipping was over, and trade was soon in a worse condition than before the war.

After a short time, I loaded a cargo of slates in Portmadoc for Cork at a very low freight and I shall never forget the feeling of relief I had when we motored out to sea over the bar. I felt like a prisoner being let out of prison. There was not the thrill I had expected in having the auxiliary, for it took all the pleasure of sailing away and the drag of the propeller deadened the vessel's way. Our speed was about four miles per hour in a calm, and it was difficult to keep the ship as clean with all the oil and grease about. But it was as well that we had the engine, for merchants would now no longer charter vessels that depended on sail alone.

CHAPTER XI

*Ireland and the Troubles – Moorhill Quay – Youghal Light –
I purchase the ketch* Irene *– also the schooner* Camborne *– Limerick
– Valentia Island – a lull in the fighting*

IN THE LATTER PART OF 1921, TRADE IN OUR CLASS OF vessel had come almost to standstill, and we were glad to accept anything that offered, whatever the freight might be. We had discharged a cargo at Gloucester, and try where I would, I could not fix up anywhere. At last, I 'phoned an agent in Newport, Mon., asking him had he anything to offer, and his reply was, nothing apart from a cargo to a place in Ireland, where if I took it I could possibly be shot. I asked him to name the place and he replied that it was Moorhill Quay in County Waterford. He also informed me that the freight was 42s. per ton, and as the current rate was only 17s., this was a very high rate indeed. Things of course were very difficult in Ireland at this time, with the 'troubles'.

I accepted the cargo, for Moorhill was a place where I had previously done quite a lot of trading, and the people there, who I knew well, were a friendly lot. I had little fear that I would be molested. When we arrived at Newport to load, I asked the agent why he had warned me of possible trouble. In reply he related how, a few weeks ago, a captain (who incidentally, I knew well) was discharging at Moorhill Quay and one day on going to the town, got himself involved in a political argument. Foolishly, he expressed the opinion that if he was in power in England, he would soon settle their affairs for them. The same evening, after dark, a number of local men went aboard his vessel and called him to come on deck. When he did so, one of the men pushed a revolver into his ribs, and ordered him to go ashore. Then, they marched him up a lane and told him to wait until their Commandant should arrive. The captain asked what did they intend to do with him. 'The Commandant, when he arrives, will decide,' they said, 'and he will probably give orders for you to be shot.' Two hours went by. No Commandant arrived. The men either got tired of waiting, or more likely, they thought the captain had had enough punishment and so they released him. Now, writing about Ireland forty years or so later, I must say, that in all my years of trading, I have never in any circumstances had any cause to choose my words in conversation with anyone. Everyone there showed me such kindness, and some even paid me the compliment of saying they were sure I must be Irish myself.

I mentioned earlier how during the war years, a merchant in southern Ireland, had sold a cargo of oats to Plymouth, although I had given him no option to send us there, and how I had taken the cargo to save trouble. This merchant's quays and stores were a couple of miles higher up the river from Moorhill, and when he heard that I was discharging at the 'Quay', he sent his son to call on me with an invitation for me to visit him at his home. I accepted his invitation, and although we had parted pretty bad friends, he seemed to have forgotten all about it and greeted me warmly. He reminded me that it was four years since I had done business with him. 'How was it,' he enquired, 'I had not offered him my vessel? Would I load for him when I got back to the Bristol Channel?'

'Yes,' I said, 'and what freight do you offer?'

'Will you be satisfied if I pay you the same rate as you have now?' he asked.

'The freight on the cargo I am now discharging is 42s,' I stated.

'That is all right,' he said, 'we will fix you up at that rate.'

I did not feel too comfortable over this deal, for I felt that I had taken an unfair advantage over our last deal together and I had no wish to do this although he was a rich man. However, I loaded the cargo and when it was discharged and I had made out the freight note, I thought, 'I must knock off two shillings per ton for it is altogether too much'. When I presented the note, he said it was damned decent of me to be so considerate. I myself was not so sure.

In November of that year (1921), we were at Dungarvan, discharging coal for the Gas Company. Earlier in the month, the Royal Irish Constabulary had been disbanded with no police force formed to take their place and enforce the law. We had all stopped work at midday for dinner, and were having our meal, when I heard the sound of our hand winch at work. I went on deck to see what was happening and to my amazement, saw several carts on the quayside, waiting their turn to load with coal from our cargo. Men were down the hold, filling the coal into baskets while others were at the winch, heaving them to load the waiting carts. They were quite openly stealing our coal. I asked what they were doing, and ordered them to stop, but they took no notice. I hastened to the merchant to tell him he was being robbed, but he only shrugged his shoulders and remarked that he had no power to stop them. I had never realised before how necessary it was to have a police force.

Our trading was now mainly to the south of Ireland and there were many risks in the winters in these deeply laden vessels. Sometimes, to enable us to make our trips, we would keep to the weather shore with a southerly wind, passing close to Lundy Island and setting a course for Roches Point. Very often, after running the distance by the log, mist would obscure the land and the lights, and for safety we would lay to until the mist cleared. It was a most wretched experience to lay to in a big sea for hours on end, waiting to make a light in the darkness or the land in daytime.

I remember one occasion on a trip from Barry with coal for Youghal. After leaving Barry the weather deteriorated, with a strong southerly wind and driving mist. By midnight we had run the distance by the log, and I brought the *Kate* to the wind, to lay to until the mist cleared. Not a nice prospect; to have run the distance and then to be unable to make your port.

We had hardly brought the vessel to, when I made Ballycotton light. Now, would it be clear enough to make the light at Youghal[1]? Even in clear weather it was a difficult light to pick out from those of the town, and it was essential to make this light so that we could approach on a safe bearing to enter harbour. Fortunately, in no time, we made the light and came safely to anchor. I can well remember the satisfaction we felt in getting to anchor on this occasion after the rolling and tossing outside.

Another nasty experience I recall was during the month of May, at a time when we do not expect heavy gales. We were coming down Channel. The sun was showing a big ring and was almost obscured, the barometer was falling, and when we were abreast of St. Govan's lightship, my mate said to me, 'Skipper, that is a nasty looking sky; it looks as if we are in for a gale of wind.'

We had been windbound for quite a long time before this trip and were anxious to make our passage. As the wind was fair, I passed Milford Haven, where, if I had sought shelter, we would have been in quite soon. But we carried on, and the wind steadily increased, until the gale blew with such force and the sea rose so high that I thought our schooner would founder. We ran back for Milford, and with the amount of water on the deck, we were lucky by the time we were to anchor that our vessel did not sink under us. A lot of the bulwark was washed away, and sails were blown away to the value of about a hundred pounds.

During 1922 I purchased the lovely ketch *Irene* and felt proud to be the owner of this quite new ship. She had very fine lines and was fitted with an auxiliary engine. Built in Bridgwater for Messrs. Colthurst Symons, she was named after Miss Irene Symons. My wife's second brother, Captain Ira Aldridge, became her master. In June 1922, I also bought a second vessel the schooner *Camborne*, from the Hook Colliery Co., of Haverfordwest. They had purchased her, along with several other coasting vessels in 1920 at a big price, to carry their anthracite to continental ports. They fitted an auxiliary engine in the *Camborne* at considerable expense, and took down her square topsail yards, so making her into a fore-and-aft rigged schooner. When the government stopped the export of coal, the colliery company had no further use for these vessels they had so recently bought and the whole fleet was laid up for sale.

I put my brother, Captain William Shaw, in charge of my faithful old *Kate* and with a fresh crew I joined the *Camborne* where she lay in the Haverfordwest river.

My first trip in her was from Gloucester to Limerick with a cargo of bacon-curing salt. I was interested to see how she handled under sail alone and hardly used the auxiliary. We had strong head winds, with a bit of rough sea on the passage, and I was very pleased with how the *Camborne* behaved as a sea boat, and with her fine sailing qualities.

It was evening when we moored alongside the quay at Limerick. The Shannon pilot, who had boarded us at Scattery Island, went ashore to stay the night in a house where the Scattery Island pilots lodged until they could get a passage back home on an outward bound boat. After a few hours he returned and came aboard to ask my permission to stay the remainder of the night on my ship. It appeared that several men, belonging to a political party, had com-

Another view on board the schooner Camborne.

Coasting schooners in Penarth Roads, May 1930.

The Bridgwater-built ketch Irene, *bought by Captain Shaw in 1922.*

Schooners and other coasting vessels windbound in Menai Straits, about 1900.

mandeered the house and had ordered him to get out. This was right at the beginning of the fighting in Limerick between the Government of the Irish Free State and the Irish Republican Army.

After discharging our salt cargo, we loaded flour for Fenit, in Tralee Bay. We left Limerick, landed the pilot back on Scattery Island, and then motored out of the mouth of the Shannon. There was a big Atlantic swell but the wind had dropped to a calm. We found it necessary to stop the engine as the circulating pump had gone wrong and the cylinders were overheating. The *Camborne*, with the way off her, was rolling about and making it difficult for us to find the fault in the pump. A thick mist had set in and visibility got so poor that we lost Loop Head Light, although we were close to it. It was no use running to leeward for Fenit until it made a clearing, and so we stood to sea on the starboard tack. A breeze sprang up from the north east and was soon blowing a gale, the mist turning to heavy rain. We shortened sail, and spent the next twenty-four hours battering against a fierce northerly gale. It was unbelievable that we could have such a gale in the month of July.

As the next day wore on, the wind shifted more to the west. Most of our sails had been blown away and all we had left whole by this time was the double reefed mainsail—which was a new one—and a couple of headsails. We were now on a lee shore with the engine still out of action and only the mainsail set. A big sea was running. The high mountains of Kerry were under the lee and we could just make out Valentia Island, so I kept the *Camborne* away for the harbour.

She was easy to steer if the auxiliary engine was working and the propeller turning, but without the auxiliary she was very different. She was slow to answer the helm, and to enter this harbour, with its narrow entrance, with the small amount of sail we had set, was a very risky undertaking.

It was dark by the time we got to the entrance. There are two leading lights to guide vessels in, and there is no danger if these are kept in line, but this night, with mountainous seas following, the *Camborne* would yaw from one side of the channel to the other. I would put the helm hard over the moment she would start on another yaw, towards the other side, but I was afraid we would crash into the rocks before there was any response to the helm.

Massive waves were breaking against the rocks on either side, leaving the water a mass of boiling foam; my crew, who were watching from both sides of the vessel as we passed through the narrowest part, would call out, in turn, 'Skipper! we are in the breakers this side.'

We were thankful indeed when we were safely at anchor in the calmer water off Knight's Town.

It took most of the next day to get things back in order. We replaced the sails that were torn and I found that the trouble with the circulating pump had been caused by a piece of metal underneath a valve. As soon as the gale died down, we started up the engine and sailed, and a few hours later we were at Fenit pier. Then we began discharging and found that some of the flour had been damaged by sea water, caused by wedges holding the hatch tarpaulin being washed away. This damaged flour I agreed to take back to Limerick, where it could be dealt with. In any case we were returning, for I had agreed to trade with the millers there. At this time all Ireland was very short of flour, for railway tracks had been torn up, most roads blocked and ships were hard to get, and few vessels cared to trade there at this time. The Limerick millers were grateful to me for my offer to trade.

Arriving in the Shannon, we failed to get a pilot at Scattery Island so carried on to the next pilot station, on Grass Island. A pilot came off to me but he was reluctant to board us, and begged me to anchor until things were more normal in Limerick. I thought he was exaggerating so I insisted we carry on. But I soon found out who was right. As we came alongside the quays we found the flour mill from which we were to load occupied by troops. They were firing across the river at Cleeves' factory, while a hail of bullets was coming back across to the mill from there as well as from the Strand Barracks by the bridge. We quickly tied up and were glad to get below. Our pilot cleared off and I never saw him again.

We could not have chosen a worse place for our berth was right in line of fire, and what the men were firing at, I do not think they knew. I believe the *Camborne* got more than a fair share of the bullets. We had them in the hull, the masts and the rigging and this shooting went on sporadically for days.

The whole of Limerick, apart from this shooting, was like a city of the dead. No one moved in the streets, and all shops and businesses were at a standstill. We became very short of bread and meat, and by some means or other, I cannot remember how, a rumour spread that there would be a lull in the fighting for a few hours, to enable civilians to get a supply of bread and what provisions they could. This lull was to start at 11.00 a.m.

When the hour came, I asked two of my crew to go to the bakehouse, but they refused to go, and said they were not leaving the ship, bread or no bread.

However, I did not intend to miss this chance, so I set off with a shopping bag in my hand. I did not know where the bakehouse was but I expected to see someone who could direct me. When I got to the street I found it quite deserted, with not a person in sight. Passing a house, with its door partly open, I called out, 'Is anyone in?' A man appeared. I told him I had come off a ship and I wished to know the way to a bakehouse. He informed me I would have to cross the bridge to find one but he advised me not to go and to return to my ship. But I started for the bridge, there still being no sign of life anywhere. On my way I noticed that most of the doors were barricaded and the windows sandbagged. Then I saw two women running towards me, they asked me, 'Was I going for bread?' I replied that I was, only I did not know where to find the bakehouse. They said that was just the place where they were going and would I let them walk with me, for they were sure if I would, they would be quite safe. I could see they were very frightened. I told them to come along and not to be alarmed, and I assured them that no Irishman would shoot a woman in the street. As we walked along I explained that I was an Englishman and was confident that we would come to no harm.

When we reached the bakehouse, a lot of people were there being served with bread and I obtained several loaves. I put them in my bag, slung it over my shoulder, and waved goodbye to the two women, who now seemed quite happy.

On my way back, I thought that I might be able to buy a ham or some bacon. So I made my way to a part of the city where the provision shops were, on the chance that one might be open. I was lucky! Looking through the window I saw a fine ham hanging up in a shop, the door of which was partly open. I entered and asked the shopkeeper if he would sell me the ham. He let me have it, but when I asked how much he said he did not care whether I paid him or not. Things were much too serious in Ireland to worry about money at this time. Having paid him, I put the ham in my bag along with the bread, and set off again, this time down a side street on my way back to the *Camborne*.

Then, for the first time that day I felt alarmed. Part of the way down the street, on the side where I was walking, I had to step off the pavement to avoid stepping into a large pool of fresh blood. Just beyond, on the same side, I saw two men, standing by a house armed with rifles held at the ready. From the house, leading to a hole in the centre of the road were two lines of covered wire and I thought to myself, 'These men are guarding a mine!' I realised it was no use for me to turn and go back. I stepped back on to the pavement and passed close to the men. They looked at me but did not speak. I kept my eyes on the end of the street, where I believed I would be safe, once I had turned the corner. I did not hurry. Nothing happened. It was a dangerous time.

I got back aboard the *Camborne*. The shooting had not restarted, and as it was nearing high water, I decided to shift from where we were and enter the dock, which was some distance down the river, well away from the rifle and machine-gun fire. We moved to the river side of the dock, and there we were quite isolated. It was a relief, I thought, to be clear of the shooting.

We were lying alongside our new berth there, the vessel's rail being about two feet below the level of the quay wall, and were busy about the deck, when suddenly a hail of bullets went whistling between our masts, striking the ground like hailstones and causing the dust to rise alongside us. I called to the crew to get down and hurriedly went below myself in a very worried state of mind. I asked myself, 'Were they shooting at us?' sitting there for some time until at last the occasional bursts of shooting stopped. I then went on deck to look for my crew and had to laugh when I discovered two of them lying at the bottom of the hold almost completely covered with sacks of damaged flour. They were hopefully using the sacks as a shield against any bullets that might come their way. They were very angry with me for laughing at them and blamed me for all the risks to which we had been exposed. Later I discovered that this outburst of shooting had not been directed at us but at some other target and we just happened to have been close to their line of fire.

Within another couple of days the shooting was over in Limerick. The government forces brought an eighteen-pounder gun into action and the first object they bombarded was the Strand Barracks. After about four hours, the fighting was over as far as Limerick was concerned. The next day the city came back to life. Shops opened, business was resumed and we moved back to our original berth ready to commence loading.

We had no trouble in getting to Caherciveen which is a port just off Valentia Harbour. Our pilot lived on a small island there. He was very friendly and took it upon himself to look after me as well as pilot my vessel safely. When he came out to us, he brought me a lovely griddle seed cake and every time he was our pilot thereafter he never failed to bring me one. He also went to great pains to warn me to be very careful what I said or did in Ireland at this time reminding me the times were dangerous.

---

1 Youghal Light was later altered to a flashing light, much more easily distinguishable with red sectors over the dangers.

CHAPTER XII

Trading round Ireland – Killorglin – 'This vessel sunk by rebels' – bacon for Liverpool – engine trouble on the Camborne

WE CONTINUED TO TRADE BETWEEN VARIOUS IRISH ports, and trade being slack on the English coast it was not long before my other two vessels, the *Kate* and the *Irene* arrived to trade with me.

All this time, I had received no letters from Arlingham and the only letters I had been able to get through had been put aboard one of our armed trawlers. The Irish banks were closed and our freights being paid by cheque, we had to hold them until they would resume business again. I also held the payments from my other two vessels, and after a few months trading with the three vessels, I was holding quite a lot of cash value in cheque form.

We had some unusual cargoes. The captain of the *Irene* had chartered to go with a general cargo from Tralee round to Dingle. Arriving in the latter port he loaded a number of live pigs back to Tralee, the animals being loose in the hold and earth ballast having been spread there for the pigs to stand on. What would have happened had our ketch encountered bad weather going out round The Blaskets does not bear thinking of. But the pigs came to no harm and the buyers were more than pleased, especially so with the extra price they obtained from the bacon curers on account of the scarcity of meat and the difficulty of moving any pigs.

It was now October. One Sunday evening, when my vessel was in her usual loading berth in Limerick, ready to sail again for Fenit, a private from the Free State Army came aboard. Informing me that his Commanding Officer wished to see me, he asked me to accompany him. The soldier took me aboard a paddle boat. This boat I knew had been purchased some time before as a venture, to run pleasure trips from Limerick to different places down the River Shannon. The Free State Government, having commandeered her, had put an ex-Sergeant Major, who was an Englishman, in charge as Lieutenant, and he was the Commanding Officer who had sent for me. I was announced, and I stood before him for some time, he taking no notice of me. He was intent on a rifle across his knees, of which he was repeatedly opening and shutting the bolt and pulling the trigger.

'Well!' I said at last, 'do you want to speak to me?'

He looked up then and asked me, 'How long will it take to get up steam?'

'We are a motor vessel,' I replied.

'Well, how long will it take you to get your ship ready to sail?'

'Why do you ask me?' I enquired.

'Never mind asking questions,' he said, 'we are commandeering your ship tonight, so you must keep your crew aboard. That is all you need to know.'

I went back aboard the *Camborne*. I did not fancy going on one of their fighting expeditions, and my wooden vessel had little protection against bullets. I had not been aboard long, before a military staff car pulled up alongside, and the Paddle-Steamer Commanding Officer got out accompanied by an Officer of superior rank. They came aboard and asked me could they inspect the hold. (The hold was about eighty feet long by about twenty feet broad.) We took off some hatches and put a ladder in position for them to go down. The hold smelt strongly of damp sour flour and the senior officer was evidently not favourably impressed with it. I asked him if it was too much to enquire why he needed my vessel?

'No,' he replied, 'I will tell you. Things are not going well with us in Cork at the moment, and I have received orders from my headquarters in Dublin, to put three hundred troops aboard the first powered vessel in Limerick, and to proceed immediately to Cork.'

'Sir,' I protested, 'this ship is useless for carrying troops. It is out of the question; it would be better to wait until a steamer arrives.'

'Captain,' he replied, 'I agree this ship is not very satisfactory, but she is the only powered ship at the moment in Limerick. I find it difficult to know what to do, but orders are orders.' And with that the two of them went ashore and drove away.

Next morning, the manager of the flour mill asked what had the military come to see me about last evening, and when I explained the reason for their visit, he laughed at the thought of the *Camborne* as a troopship. I added that I had advised the officer in charge to wait until a steamer arrived. 'Then we can start loading,' he said.

We had loaded about fifty tons of flour and several lorries were waiting with more loads to ship, when the Commanding Officer of the paddle boat came back on the scene. He was very angry and demanded to know why I had commenced loading, not having had his permission to do so. He ordered us to stop and said he had fresh orders for me. We were to leave Limerick with as many troops as we could carry—in the hold, on the deck or in any place they could get—together with their stores, and land them aboard a steamer, several miles down the Shannon off Bay Castle. Government forces had stopped this steamer as she was on her way to Limerick. A non-commissioned officer would come aboard and remain with me. With him I was to proceed to Kilrush, and there to escort a small river steamer, the *Coronia* to Fenit. When I had carried out these operations, on arrival at Fenit, the *Coronia* and my vessel were to embark as many troops as we could carry and bring them back to Limerick.

Within a short space of time, several army lorries drew up on the quay alongside us, and began to load us with food supplies and about a ton of newspapers, which they lowered on top of the flour. Then the troops came aboard with their N.C.O., occupying all the decks, the hold and our living quarters. I was ordered to sail but did not intend to start on this trip on just a word-of-mouth order. I told the N.C.O. that before I left the quay, I must have orders written out and signed by the Commanding Officer, that my fuel tanks must be replenished and the military authorities must bear the cost.

After some demur I got what I asked for, and we sailed. We came to Bay Castle, lay alongside the waiting steamer and the troops clambered aboard her, the N.C.O. staying aboard my vessel. The Commanding Officer was on the steamer in charge of operations. When some of the stores had been taken aboard the steamer, the C.O. called to me, 'All right', he said, 'you can proceed now,' and to the N.C.O. standing on our deck he remarked, 'If that diehard skipper of the *Coronia* refuses to obey your order, shoot the b——.'

We started down the Shannon and after proceeding several miles down river we saw the little *Coronia* on her way up to Limerick. I said to the N.C.O. who was standing beside me. 'Well, here is your boat. I will blow the fog horn to attract their attention, then you can give her captain your orders.'

'No!' he exclaimed, 'you give the orders, I will have nothing to do with it.'

The captain of the *Coronia* turned his vessel in the direction we were heading and came alongside. He asked what we had to say. I told him the Officer standing by me had orders for him from the military headquarters in Limerick, to accompany us immediately to Fenit. The captain was terribly worried. He was carrying many passengers. Open spaces on the deck were filled with men, women and children while other parts of the deck was piled high with crates of live hens and ducks. The hatches were off and on the bottom of the vessel's hold were as many live pigs as could stand. This boat was the only means of transport at this time, for roads were blocked and no trains running.

When the passengers heard the orders I had for the captain, they were dumbfounded and some became angry. They were very concerned at the thought of a trip to a place where there could be no transport to get them back home. One man came aboard my vessel and asked me was I English. When I replied that I was, he said. 'How dare you come here and order people about. We have had enough of your sort in this country.'

The captain then asked me how could he obey this order considering his passengers and cargo.

I replied, 'You must do as you please.'

'Right! I will,' he said, and turned his boat in the direction of Limerick and continued on his way.

During the night we landed alongside Fenit Pier and the N.C.O. left the ship. After breakfast, I went to the barracks to find out what their instructions were. They knew nothing and were not interested in us. Most of the stores we had taken aboard in Limerick were still in the hold on top of the flour, and people began to come along and help themselves. So I paid another visit to the barracks to advise them what was happening to their stores but they took little or no notice of me.

The railway line from Fenit to Tralee was not open on account of sabotage, and Fenit pier was full of all kinds of merchandise, consigned to Tralee. Some of it was perishable, lying under tarpaulins. As soon as the merchants in Tralee heard that a vessel was in Fenit, they came down to try and charter us to shift these goods by water, up the river and canal. I was just as anxious as they were to fix a charter for my vessel but it all depended on the military. As far as I could see, there was no intention of troops being put aboard my ship for Limerick.

These merchants were people of some importance, and I told them they should approach the military to try and get my vessel released. This suggestion was of no avail for they could find no one to whom they could appeal, and the most they could do, was to get permission to discharge the part cargo of flour consigned to them.

After that we just lay waiting for orders from someone. Then, one evening, a man in civilian clothes with a revolver in his hand came down the cabin and told me to sail immediately. I was a little alarmed at first, but looking at the man I could see that he was in a very distressed state. I asked him to put his revolver down, which he did; then he sat down and proceeded to tell me what had happened to distress him. It appears that he was on his way to see me, travelling in a car with a friend, when they were ambushed and his friend who was sitting beside him was shot and killed. He insisted that I sail immediately. I told him this was impossible as I was under orders from the military authorities and I could not sail unless I had written authority from them to do so. He went ashore with nothing agreed upon.

I did not see him until next morning, when he brought a note from the military authorities ordering me to return with him to Limerick. He enquired when breakfast would be served and I told him we would have breakfast as soon as we were clear of the pier, but by then the vessel was rolling and tossing in the swell and our passenger had lost all interest in food, and he lay on the settee in the cabin until we reached the Shannon and smooth waters. Arriving in Limerick I now received letters from home. My wife was very worried about me, for the press had been full of all sorts of happenings and quite a lot of them were exaggerated. I was sorry to have caused my family so much alarm and I decided to leave this troubled part of the Irish coast and trade nearer home. I explained this to the shippers. They were sorry to lose the *Camborne*, for we had done them good service, and to help me along they loaded us with a cargo of wheat for Cork.

We had hardly moored the vessel on arrival there, when two

merchants approached me with the offer of a good freight for a round trip to Limerick and back. I told them I was not interested, and whatever freight they offered me I would not accept it.

'Oh come now,' they said, 'surely if we offer you enough freight you will accept.' I refused, and although they increased their offer, I still refused. At last, they doubled their first offer, and as I had the vessel to make a living with, I felt it would be foolish not to accept. They were very pleased with my acceptance and promised an extra ten pounds if we were back in Cork in a week's time. From here, I could get letters home without any trouble, and I wrote to my wife assuring her that things were not as bad as the reports were made out to be. I was making only one more trip before I would return home.

We had a fine trip to the Shannon, arriving off Scattery Island in the evening. One of the pilots boarded us but he was not keen to proceed at once, saying it would be advisable to anchor until daylight. I asked him why, and he said he thought there was a danger that we would be fired upon as we passed up the river in the darkness. As it was some distance to Limerick I did not want to anchor, so we sailed on. All went well until we were passing Tarbet. There was sufficient light to see a paddle steamer at anchor there, and I recognised it as the one of my friend the Commanding Officer. As we passed close to it a burst of machine-gun fire came whistling through our masts though without doing any damage. I was at a loss to understand why they should fire at us in this way, when we were near enough to them to be hailed. The tide runs fast through the narrows at this point on the Shannon by Tarbet, and with the *Camborne* motoring fast, it would be only a matter of minutes before we would follow a bend in the river, and then the land between us and Tarbet would hide us from their sight. The pilot became very alarmed and hastened to remind me that we should have anchored until daylight.

We were treated to another two bursts of fire from their machine gun but again without damage and then we were out of sight. It was not long before I saw the paddle steamer coming after us, as fast as she could steam. I eased my engine to slow, and she was soon abreast. The Commanding Officer hailed us and asked why I had not stopped when he had fired. I replied that it was for that very reason I had kept going as fast as I could. For two pins, he replied, he would shoot every man aboard us and in return I shouted that that was a very pleasant greeting to receive. He was furious at this and ordered us to alter course and return to Tarbet Roads. We did this with the paddle steamer leading the way. He came to anchor when we reached Tarbet, and ordered me to put my vessel alongside his boat. Now a paddle steamer is an awkward craft to get alongside, and with the darkness and a strong ebb tide running, I told him it would be best if we anchored first, and then he could bring his boat alongside us. But he refused to agree to this.

When we were safely alongside, he ordered me to bring the manifest of my cargo. As I stepped aboard I was met by men in uniform with their rifles at the ready, and was marched to the cabin where the Commanding Officer was waiting to receive me. 'You can think yourself a lucky man we did not shoot you and your crew,' he said.

He ignored my remark that it would have been simpler for him to have hailed us and continued: 'We have been waiting here two days for you to arrive. We knew you loaded your cargo from an American ship and we believe you had a very good freight for it but you may not be aware that you are carrying contraband for the rebels. Give me the manifest.' I handed it to him.

After a while, scanning the manifest, he exclaimed, 'Ah! "Metal Polish" is it?'

He drew my attention to items marked "Cases of Metal Polish". 'What,' he asked, 'are the "Cases of Metal Polish" for?'

I answered; 'If you read the directions, you will see it is to polish brass.'

'Yes,' he said, 'and you will laugh on the other side of your face when these cases are opened in Limerick.'

He put an armed guard aboard and the following morning we were once again on our way. At Limerick we discharged our cargo and a number of cases were duly opened. But no ammunition was found, only the cases of metal polish as per the manifest. We were back in Cork inside the week and I collected the extra ten pounds.

As soon as I entered my agents office in Cork, he turned to a man who was in the office with him and said, 'Here is the man who will take your cargo.'

This man represented a milling company and asked me would I

load for Killorglin. This I knew was a very awkward place to get to, and very few captains would consider going there. Feeling the same way about it, I said I would not go there for..... and mentioned a most exorbitant rate of freight. To my surprise, he answered immediately that he would give it.

I was taken aback by his offer and hesitated for a while before replying. I certainly did not like the idea of fixing for a place so difficult to get to, but taking into account the value of the freight, I agreed and signed the charter. Later, speaking to some people who knew Killorglin well, they told me I would be lucky if I brought my vessel away from there, as it was more than likely that the men who would act as pilots for Killorglin would put my vessel ashore where she would become a wreck, so they could steal the cargo. As I was fixed for the voyage it was really no use worrying, but as we loaded the cargo I began to think I was heading for trouble.

Next morning, on entering the agent's office to sign the Bills of Lading, he enquired had I seen the shipper of the cargo. He told me that in the morning's paper, was an account of how the rebels had stolen the cargo of a vessel discharging in Killorglin after attacking it with gunfire. As we talked, the merchant came in and as soon as he saw me he said, 'Thank goodness you haven't sailed. It is out of the question for you to take this cargo to Killorglin; will you take it to Tralee instead?'

I agreed to do so and I was even more relieved than he was that the cargo should be diverted in this way. The merchant asked my permission to send a salesman with us to dispose of the cargo, and when he arrived, I was ready to sail. On my way to the *Camborne* I met a merchant who I knew from Tralee. I enquired how he was. 'Oh', he said, 'I am in a proper fix. I had to come here on important business and I see no way of returning home. No trains are running and all the main roads are blocked'.

'Well', I said, 'you can come with us if you like, for we are leaving immediately for Tralee with a cargo of flour.'

He could hardly believe that what he heard was true. Neither he nor his wife forgot the help I gave him to get home, and they gave me a standing welcome to visit them at any time whenever I should be in the vicinity.

When we arrived at Fenit, the harbour master had alarming news for me, to the effect that my ketch the *Irene* had been sunk by the rebel forces and she was lying outside the canal gates near Tralee. He informed me that a photograph of her had appeared in a local newspaper. Our other vessel, the *Kate*, was moored close to the *Irene* I knew, and I asked the Harbour Master was she safe. But about her we had no information, and at this I was worried even more. It is about nine miles from Fenit up to Tralee. I hired a horse and trap, which cost me quite a lot of money, and set off to see for myself what damage had been done. When I neared Tralee, to my great relief, I found that both the *Kate* and the *Irene* were safe. Rumour had the wrong vessel and the one that had been sunk was a local barge of about twenty tons burthen.

I then went to the Agent's office in Tralee and met both my captains, my brother-in-law Ira of the *Irene* and my brother William of the *Kate* there. They told me that both vessels were fixed to load cargoes of bacon for Liverpool. They had to shift to Fenit to load the next morning, and sailed down there on that evening's tide. Next morning, the two of them were asked if they would cancel the charter to load the cargoes, being offered instead the estimated amount of freight as compensation. The reason for this was that when the vessels were chartered earlier the company who usually carried the bacon had no steamer available to carry that week's shipment. They could now provide their own vessel to load the consignment and so made this offer to pay. Captain Aldridge, on the *Irene* asked my advice. As he was sailing the vessel on a share basis, I felt it was for him as master to decide what he should do. He accepted the offer and the charter was cancelled.

Captain Shaw on the *Kate* next informed me of the similar offer made to him. Although it was November, the weather was good with light winds, and I advised him to take advantage of this fine spell and make his trip. Accordingly, he sailed, and arrived in Liverpool, with the cargo in good order, in just under four days. The Co-operative Wholesale Society, the shippers and receivers of the cargo, were delighted to have their consignment shipped so quickly, and at a freight that was only a fraction of that paid to the Steamship Company. These shipments were made about every ten days, and as a result the bacon curers were anxious to charter one or other of my vessels. We were confident that the *Camborne* being engined with twice the horse power of the *Kate* and a much finer schooner, would make as good or better time than she had done. When I fixed our first cargo, the weather was fine but by the time the bacon was ready to be shipped, it had changed for the worse. The wind was a strong south easterly wind, contrary for us all the way. It was no good trying to cancel the charter for that would have cost me my freight, but what was going to happen to this hundred tons of mild cured bacon, if these winds lasted? There was little doubt it would be ruined. The last part of the cargo was to be several hundredweights of sausages and these I absolutely refused to take on board, although I was assured they would keep for a week.

We sailed from Fenit just as soon as the cargo was aboard. With anything less perishable aboard I would not have sailed at all. After battling against wind and weather round Slea Head and the Blaskets in terrible conditions we were compelled to seek shelter in Valentia, as we could make no real progress.

The wind eased after we had lain there for two days but did not shift. Nevertheless we got under way and struggled against wind and sea until we were off Queenstown. Conditions had got worse again and we had to put in again for shelter. It was now a week since we had left Fenit and the thought that our entire cargo would be ruined was a great worry to me.

The next day the wind shifted to the west and we got the anchor up and under way at four p.m. I went below after we had cleared the harbour, for the engine was labouring. I felt the crankcase and I found that we had run one of the big-end bearings. The engine was a two stroke diesel, with cylinders twelve inches in diameter. A new bearing would have to be fitted at once to put the engine in working order. This was a piece of additional bad luck when we were so anxious to get this cargo to its destination.

I went on deck and told the mate, who was steering, he would have to remain at the wheel until I had fitted the new bearing. I left him in charge of the deck, while I and an A.B. set about the repairs. First we had to remove the head, a very heavy casting, and then hold up the piston while we removed the burned-out bearing. The crankcase was full of white metal, which had to be cleared, and we also found the shaft was scored. It was twenty four hours before I got the bearing running satisfactorily. All this time the mate remained at the wheel, without any relief and without any thought of complaint. We were abreast of the Skerries, off Holyhead, when I relieved him.

We duly arrived in the Mersey. The consignee had been worried over the delay in our arrival and I was glad to know that my cargo was considered to be in fairly good condition. But there was no doubt at all that my vessel would be the last schooner that would carry a cargo of bacon from Tralee to Liverpool!

The schooner Ryelands, built at Lancaster and owned for many years at Connah's Quay. She was owned by Captain Shaw for some years during World War II and was sold in 1946. Later she was converted for filming.
[Photo: Flintshire Record Office]

The end of the little schooner Elizabeth Hyam *off Ramsey in the Isle of Man, April 1925. Some years prior to this, she had been Captain Shaw's first command.*

The motor coaster Eldorita, *bought by Captain Shaw after he retired from the sea in 1946. She foundered in the North Sea in 1966.*

CHAPTER XIII

On board the Camborne – *Paulo, the dog* – *a storm at Arthurstown* – *a gale in 1927* – *the loss of the* Excel – *in Gloucester*

WE WERE LIKE A HAPPY FAMILY ON BOARD THE *Camborne*. I had shipped an A.B. in Plymouth in 1923 and he remained with me for ten and a half years. The mate, who joined my vessel in 1922, stayed with me for eight years. Both had been at sea all their lives and were fine seamen. The mate was a fine powerful man and he thought it was his special duty to see that fresh hands who were shipped paid me proper respect.

One sailor I shipped in Wexford asked my permission to bring his dog with him, and the dog became part of my crew. He was a bull terrier named 'Paulo' and was the most intelligent animal I have ever seen. He seemed to understand almost every word that was spoken to him and was friendly to all on board. Anyone belonging to the ship could handle him and take him ashore. We believed that at some time he had been the companion of a thief, for if he was taken into a shop and an article silently pointed out to him, after leaving the premises and being given the order to 'fetch', he would dash off and in due course return with the selected article.

This seaman left us after a month or so, leaving his dog behind, and my A.B. then adopted Paulo. He began to teach him some tricks, the favourite one being to put his own red knitted cap on the dog's head and his pipe in the dog's mouth, the animal meanwhile sitting up on his hind legs and remaining in this position until both hat and pipe were removed. This trick was usually done when alongside a quay, with passers-by as audience to watch Paulo perform.

My A.B. was fond of spending his evenings in the local, and it was fine fun for him to take the dog ashore and to make bets with his acquaintances that he could leave his pipe on a seat, point out the pipe to the dog, leave the pub and a little later, send Paulo back for the pipe. Quite a few drinks were collected in this way. Then came the last day aboard for our canine friend.

We had finished loading whitening in the Sussex port of Newhaven and the *Camborne* was in a shocking state with the white dust of our cargo everywhere. The mate and the A.B. and the dog were all in a bad humour. The two men were drawing water with buckets from over the side for sluicing and washing the decks, and Paulo was in their way. They ordered him time and again to move from where he was, and when he did not move fast enough he was splashed with more than a few buckets of water. Paulo showed his resentment with bad tempered growls, and this went on for some time. At last, being thoroughly fed up with this treatment, the dog jumped on to the ship's rail, climbed the vertical ladder let into the quay wall, and, reaching the quay, turned to give one fierce growl and then cleared off. We tried everywhere to find him in the vicinity but he had disappeared and there was no trace of him. To me and my crew it was like losing a friend.

In 1923, while lying windbound in Milford Haven during a period of gales, I received news that my father had died. I had a great affection for him and I would like to think that I had some of the qualities of unselfishness and kindness which I had admired so much in him. Some months later, in 1924, we brought the *Camborne* up to Gloucester for a general survey and renewed the whole of the decks. The work was undertaken by a Mr. Peterson, a Scandinavian who owned several schooners. He was a man it was a pleasure to know and to work with.

After leaving dry-dock we found that trading conditions had worsened, freights were at their lowest and cargoes of any kind difficult to secure. I tried east coast trading but found this even worse than the trade I had been on. I well recall arriving in Perth with a cargo of oil cake, at this time everyone was surprised to see a schooner there for they thought such vessels had gone out long ago. So it was that we returned to the south-west and Irish waters that I knew so well.

It happens every so often, especially during the winter months, that storms occur that are remembered for many years afterwards. At the end of 1925, we were on passage to Arthurstown, a small pier in Waterford harbour. Now, by this date all coasting schooners were old and long past their best, and it was necessary for those who sailed in these craft to use the utmost caution when venturing out during stormy periods in winter-time.

We had experienced bad weather all the passage, with strong winds from the south west and driving rain, making it impossible to see any distance. We were lucky to make the Coningbeg lightship before everything was blotted out by even thicker weather. It is eleven miles from the lightship to the Hook Light, which marks the entrance to Waterford harbour, and I did not see the Hook until we were abreast of it and then only for a short time. Had our compass been out, we could so easily have been ashore. As the water shallows quickly, it causes a big sea and the channel narrows as it reaches the treacherous Dunmore Sands on the port side and Duncannon port on the starboard. The relief we all felt in the *Camborne* when we made Duncannon was great, and we came to anchor in Passage East. The next evening we moored on the tide alongside the pier in Arthurstown.

Early the following morning we started to discharge our cargo of coal. This was hove up and tipped into a hand barrow, then wheeled ashore across a plank placed from the vessel to the quay. It was taken ashore by two men supplied by the merchant who was the receiver of the cargo.

As the day wore on, the wind began to increase in strength, until by midday it was blowing so hard that it was dangerous for the men to stand on the plank. They were afraid they would be blown off, so work was stopped. By now although it was only at low tide, the spray was coming right over the pier, and it was not hard to imagine or foresee what it would be like when the tide was in.

The *Camborne* was lying broadside to the wind. In this position it was difficult to hold her alongside and we put out extra moorings. As the tide made, so the gale increased in fury, and the spray that was breaking over the pier was now more like solid walls of water, crashing over and filling our decks. About an hour before high water, all the bow moorings parted, leaving our vessel stern on to the pier.

At high water, the deck bollard holding the stern moorings broke, and the whole of the stern rail went over the side. The *Camborne* was now adrift and she drove on to the beach, stern on to the wind. The storm blew itself out and when the next high water came, which was the top of a spring tide, it only reached the five feet mark, whereas we required eight feet to float the schooner when she was empty. It is the custom when any vessel insured at Lloyds is in trouble, for one of their agents to attend and to assess the damage, reporting the position back to London. As no agent came, I telephoned to my shipbroker, who informed me he knew about our stranding and had been in communication with Lloyds. They informed him they could not trace any record of insurance on my vessel. I was very concerned about this, and after some thought I sent my broker a telegram, enquiring who were the underwriters with whom we were insured? The reply I received from him was worded: 'Regrettable omission. Have failed to reinsure your vessel.' My shipbroker acted for a firm of insurance brokers in London who covered the vessel on a yearly premium, to be renewed annually. He had acted for me in this respect for many years and hitherto had never failed to keep the *Camborne* covered until this occasion. This was a serious situation. There was the cost of repairs and the extra expense to discharge the coal on the beach. There was also the risk of the *Camborne* being driven higher up than where she already lay and of having to dig a channel to refloat her. I required help to get anchors run out and there was the delay in waiting for the next spring tides. It was no consolation to be told that never, in the memory of anyone living in the area, had there been a storm of such severity. After considerable expense, worry and work, the *Camborne* floated off on the next spring tides and with what amounted to only minor damage.

The next severe storm we encountered was on the 28th of October 1927. We were on passage from the Mersey to Baltimore in County Cork, and had to seek shelter off Anglesey in Moelfre Roads. The wind was too strong from the south west to get the few miles to Holyhead, but I was anxious to get there for two reasons. One was that Holyhead is a safe harbour, while Moelfre Roads is not a safe anchorage, being exposed to northerly winds. My second reason was that my agent had received no cover note on the vessel's insurance, and having regard to what had happened two years before at Arthurstown I did not want to take any chances again.

We got under way in a lull on the morning of the 28th October, and leaving Moelfre Roads passed close to the auxiliary ketch *Exce* anchored there. Her master was Captain Ballance whom I knew well. He hailed me to the effect that there was too much wind to make Holyhead that day. But his remark did not deter me. My intended course was to keep close to the weather shore and pass inside the Middle and West Mouse Islands and the Skerries. The most difficult part would be from Carmel Point to Holyhead Bay and although I believed it would be a struggle, I had no fear but that we would make Holyhead safely. After passing close to Point Lynas, the wind was coming off the shore in strong gusts and it showed signs of blowing harder now than it had done for the past few days.

When we reached Carmel Point, to prepare for the struggle we double reefed the three fore and aft sails and furled the two outer jib sails, which left the vessel under very small sail. To my surprise, on looking astern, I saw the *Excel* coming along after us under all sail and with her auxiliary engine working also. Under pressure of so much sail and with the help of the auxiliary, she was soon abreast of us and to windward. To see her carrying all this canvas was a cause of great worry to me, for I felt certain that if she did not reduce sail before she opened up the sea off Carmel Point, she would meet with disaster. There is also a tide race off Carmel Point on the ebb, making conditions in bad weather even more hazardous.

The wind was still increasing in force. We watched the *Excel* clear Carmel Point and soon she was in difficulties. It seemed to me that her auxiliary had stopped. She was wallowing and rolling, and dropping fast to leeward making no effort to tack ship.

And we ourselves were now in the tide race. At first, we made some bad plunges into the breaking waves but as the way went off the *Camborne*, we did better, and as soon as we could make about, on the starboard tack, I tacked ship. It was touch and go that our old schooner came on the other tack and she buried herself in the sea when she came head to wind. The engine kept working and she was on the other tack minus the fore staysail. The further we stood in on this tack, the sooner we would be in smooth water.

The last I saw of the *Excel* was just before a rain squall blotted everything out. She was then in a bad way and dangerously near to the Skerries Rocks, to leeward of her. But we could render her no help for we had as much as we could do ourselves to make headway.

When we were about half way up the bay, I saw the Trinity House boat coming towards us. She made no effort to communicate with us; but just rounded our stern and then headed back to Holyhead. Evidently, she had been sent to our assistance and finding we were making good progress, returned to Holyhead. We came to anchor there without further incident. We let go both anchors, and snugged down. During the night the gale blew with hurricane force and the Holyhead lifeboat was called out several times to assist vessels around us who were dragging their anchors in the harbour.

The next day it was learned that a distress call had been made from the Skerries at 3.00 p.m. (October 28th) from a vessel off Carmel Point. This had been picked up by the Moelfre lifeboat, the *Charles and Eliza Laura*, which was launched immediately. This lifeboat was an old type, sailing and pulling boat, with no engine and manned by fifteen men.

They set off on this short wintry afternoon, to search for the vessel in distress and it was almost dark when the ketch *Excel* was sighted. She was a heartrending sight, her sails were in ribbons, her bulwarks gone and the seas making a clean breach over her decks.

A quick decision had to be made. Second coxswain William Roberts, who was steering, prompted by the coxswain of the lifeboat, Owen Jones, with the full approval of the gallant crew, steered the lifeboat right across the sinking vessel. For a few seconds the lifeboat lay on top of the ketch; only just long enough to get her crew aboard and then she floated off.[1]

The lifeboat was badly holed through striking the vessel and was full of water. Now began the struggle against a hurricane force wind to get the waterlogged boat back to safety. It took eighteen hours to do this with the waves constantly breaking over the boat. Eighteen hours of unbelievable hardship.

William Roberts, the sixty five years old second coxswain of the *Excel* died in the boat from exposure, and the remainder of the crew were almost exhausted when they came into port. This rescue will remain one of the outstanding examples of gallantry and heroism ever recorded in the annals of the Royal National Lifeboat Institution.

---

[1] For a fuller account of this lifeboat rescue, see WRECK AND RESCUE ON THE COAST OF WALES, VOLUME II. (1972)

CHAPTER XIV

Hard times – the Irene *and* Kate *are sold – a cargo from the wreck* Nordstad *– my sons aboard on holiday – trouble at Kilmakilloge – a voyage light from Tralee – buying Irish scrap iron*

FROM 1928 ONWARDS IT WAS EVEN MORE DIFFICULT TO find work for our vessels. When we secured a cargo we knew before we loaded that it would hardly pay our expenses, yet I was determined to hold on to the *Camborne*. I think why I was so determined, was the memory of my early days and the hard times when my father lost his command. My brother-in-law, Captain Ira Aldridge, informed me he could no longer remain master of the *Irene* and lose money, and that he would have to find other employment. Thus I was compelled to sell this vessel, receiving only half of what I paid for her. Messrs. Colthurst Symons of Bridgwater purchased her, being in fact her original owners.

The schooner *Kate* of which my brother William was master, was in the same straits. I sold her at last for four hundred and fifty pounds. This was the vessel for which I had refused two thousand five hundred pounds, and had spent a like amount to repair and fit with an engine.

Yet we were not as badly off as some in the coasting trade, and through all this time of losses and slump I have no recollection of any of my family being deprived of anything or in want; we had sufficient to eat and enough money to pay our way. Yet it was hard to understand why there should be so much distress and poverty in the world. When we were in Ireland we heard men, who had years before emigrated to America (the richest country in the world), thank God they were back in a country where they could at least have food.

Freights from the Bristol Channel to Cornish ports were now down to 3s. per ton. This moreover did not cover the cost of fuel, port charges and the crew's wages. I was lucky, I managed to charter the *Camborne* with the Irish government to carry kelp from different ports in Galway and Clare to the Iodine Works in Galway and we obtained extra freight for this work. When there was no more kelp to carry, I chartered to load scrap iron from the wreck *Nordstad*, a sailing ship that had been wrecked several years before. Loading this cargo was a risky undertaking as the remains of the wreck were exposed to the sea. We took this cargo to Connah's Quay. My son Kenneth spent his summer holidays with me on this trip to the west of Ireland and he got into a little trouble with his school head through being absent when the autumn term commenced.

We discharged the scrap iron at Messrs. Summers' wharf at Shotton, and from Connah's Quay secured a cargo of fireclay goods for Belfast. There we loaded cider apples for Cherbourg and a local newspaper reported this cargo as being the first of its kind to be shipped from Ireland to France. Had I known beforehand the trouble and discomfort this cargo was going to cause me, I would never have chartered for it.

It was now late November, and we were lucky to get to Falmouth without delay, but we had to seek shelter there as the wind was blowing strong from the south-east. The damaged and squashed apples, loaded in bulk into the hold, began to ferment, and a poisonous vapour rose from the hatches, which grew worse day by day. Ultimately the smell of it could be smelt throughout Falmouth town, people wondering wherever it could be coming from. The wind backed more to the west and was still stormy when we left Falmouth. Although it was not the weather to be sailing, I had only one desire and that was to get rid of those apples. It was blowing so hard when we were motoring into the dock at Cherbourg, the *Camborne* could hardly make steerage way, and when we tied up safely, the Dock Master expressed his surprise to me that we had received no damage on the crossing.

My three sons each in turn spent their long summer vacations from school with me, usually on trips to the west of Ireland. My eldest son Bernard was with me on the following trip of which I write. We had discharged salt in Tralee from Gloucester, and I accepted a cargo which I had been offered by telegram, to load salt mackerel in barrels at several different ports in County Kerry for Liverpool. The shipper who chartered us lived in Castletown. We proceeded to the first port for loading which was Ardgroom in Kenmare River.

It was evening when we reached the entrance to the estuary and it was blowing hard from the east. This was too strong for us to motor head to wind with a light ship. We tacked under sail, from one side to the other, with the additional help of the auxiliary, and we came to anchor abreast of Sneem. At about nine the next morning, a pilot came off in a small motor boat and boarded us. He was of the opinion that the wind was too strong to attempt the harbour. I could see Ardgroom to leeward of us and it appeared easy of access to me, there being good leading marks to enter. It really was a perfect landlocked little inlet, but with all, it was a most desolate looking place with not a house anywhere in sight. I told the pilot I could see no risk in making the attempt, and as he was willing, I told my mate to heave in the anchor chain whilst I went below and started the engine.

The mate called out that the anchor chain was short and asked me to come ahead with the engine. I put in the clutch and this was followed by the sound of a crash below. I pulled out the clutch and called to my mate to slack away the chain, then went below to investigate.

I thought at first that something had broken in the gearbox, instead I found the holding bolts in the coupling had all fallen out, and the tailend shaft was bent out of line. I was now in a serious situation; in an exposed position in the mouth of the Kenmare River with an empty ship, my engine out of order, and as far as I knew, no means of getting the vessel to a place of safety.

I came on deck and told the pilot what had happened, asking his advice about attempting to enter Ardgroom harbour to leeward under sail alone. He advised against it, but informed me that in the next little inlet, Kilmakilloge Harbour, the landlord of the inn there owned a motor fishing boat, which he thought probably had sufficient power to tow the *Camborne* into the harbour.

The next thing to be considered was how to get to him, for it was blowing too hard to attempt to reach the shore in my small boat. I asked the pilot would he take me in his motor boat so that I could make arrangements about the tow, and would he also bring me back aboard again. He agreed to do so and my son and I set off with him for Kilmakilloge.

When we arrived at the inn, the landlord's wife informed me her husband had gone to Kenmare as it was market day, and he would not be home until late afternoon. She advised us to wait in the bar and there we sat for hour after hour. My son was intrigued in watching the enjoyment with which the customers drank their glasses of frothing stout. Dinner time came, and the landlord's wife invited us to have a meal with her and her family, which we were pleased to accept. At last her husband arrived and he offered me the services of his boat at a very reasonable charge. He also advised me to bring my vessel into Kilmakilloge, and I went with him to inspect the berth and agreed to be towed there.

We berthed the *Camborne* alongside the quay at high water. I advised the shipper of the mackerel cargo what had happened, and I expressed the hope that I would be in a position to load the fish in a day or so.

The first thing we had to do was draw the tail shaft, and when the tide ebbed, we removed the propeller and tried to draw the shaft. It was impossible being too much out of straight to come through the tube.

By the next ebb, I had made all ready to draw the tube along with the shaft. With the help of, I believe, all the able men folk in the village, standing almost waist deep in water, the shaft and the tube came out. It took a mighty pull to do the job, and here I must pay tribute to everyone in Kilmakilloge for the help they gave me without any thought of reward.

A friend brought along a horse and cart, and the eighteen-foot shaft was put on the cart and taken to Kenmare. I was hoping there would be an engineering shop near, where I could put the shaft on a lathe, but there was none. However, a consultation with some blacksmiths resulted in them undertaking the job of straightening. They heated the bent shaft and set to work on it, and when finished the shaft was as straight and true as when it was first installed. It was a Thursday when we entered Kilmakilloge and everything was back in order by the following Tuesday. We left to enter Ardgroom and to commence loading, but to my surprise I found a little steamer there taking aboard my cargo. There was nothing to be done but to return to Kilmakilloge.

I was undecided what to do but went ashore and called to see my friend the landlord, to tell him what had happened. He advised me to go to Castletown and have a talk with the man who had chartered the *Camborne* and a minute later he offered to drive me there.

On meeting the shipper, I reminded him that he had chartered us by telegram to load without mention of days, and I told him I intended to hold him to the contract. He blustered a bit at first, but fortunately for us both eventually offered me another cargo of fish for Liverpool.

Living near Gloucester, I was able to fix up for most of the cargoes of salt that were shipped from the Severn to the bacon curing firms in south-western Ireland. The only trouble with this trade was the difficulty in getting back with an empty vessel. Having the auxiliary, we risked making the trips without ballast, which was taking a very big risk indeed, especially in winter.

I remember one very nasty experience I had, coming light from Tralee. The wind was fresh and off the shore, blowing off the land in strong gusts. The *Camborne*, having no ballast at all, was heeling over so far that we could hardly stand on deck, and at the same time, we were being being driven very fast to leeward. The position we were in somehow stopped the water from circulating around the cylinders, and I was forced to stop our engine. We had tacked ship off Mizzen Head, and would have fetched the entrance to Castletown on that tack, but with the engine stopped we could not hold our position in the shelter of the land and we drifted off.

We shortened sail, and for the next tack were almost on our beam ends, expecting the *Camborne* to turn over at any minute with the weight of wind and the big sea running. On this occasion it was a whole week before we got back to Mizzen Head, and then only because we were helped by a change of wind.

To avoid running these risks in the future, I arranged with a firm of scrap iron buyers from the Bristol Channel who agreed with me that if I could find dealers around the west coast of Ireland who had quantities of scrap for sale, I should inform them. They would then send a representative to buy, and I would carry the scrap for them.

We had several cargoes back by this method, but the freight paid was not very much, so I decided to buy the scrap iron myself and sell direct to the steelworks. Sometimes we were only able to buy small quantities, but still there was a little cash to be made. I was amused at one incident, buying scrap in a port in southern Ireland, where I had managed to hunt up about sixty tons. An old woman came to me with a few pounds of old iron in her hands and asked me to buy. I told her what she had would only be worth a penny or so, and I did not buy in such small quantities. But I took the iron and gave her a couple of shillings. It was not long before she came back with another few small pieces of iron.

'Now!' I said, 'look here, I told you before, I do not buy in small quantities. What you have is of no value. Here is two shillings but do not come to me again.'

Before the day was out, she was back again with another few pieces of old iron. I was feeling impatient with her by this time, and I told her to take the scrap back where she had found it.

'Sure!' she said, 'you don't begrudge a poor old widow a few shillings, and Sir, I have no one to support me. I lost my five sons at sea.'

What could I do but give the poor old woman a few more shillings.

CHAPTER XV

John Kennedy – becalmed off Land's End – on the rocks off Jersey – repairs at Par – a tragedy in the Bristol Channel – back to Ireland – salt and scrap iron

IN 1929 I HAD LOADED A CARGO OF COAL FOR THE FISHERY school at Baltimore in County Cork. This school was for the purpose of training boys in seamanship, boat building, fishing and other trades, boys who were either orphans or in need of care. I had a vacancy on the *Camborne* for a boy, and asked the old sailor who was the instructor in charge, William Nolan, if I could ship one as a member of my crew. He said I could, providing the priest in charge was willing. Having obtained the consent of the priest, a fine, well-built youth joined our vessel. This fine young man, John Kennedy, proved to be a good sailor and most trustworthy; we got on so well together that we were like father and son. Unfortunately, he had one great fault, and that was a complete disregard for his own safety. I would often caution him to be more careful, but he would only laugh and say, 'Why do you worry? I am not a child, I am well able to take care of myself.' In 1932, this young man scalded his foot, and he had to remain in hospital for treatment, this being the second time he was admitted to hospital through his own carelessness.

The previous year (1931) my second son, Humphrey Kenneth, asked to join my ship and he became a member of my crew. Although he was subject to sea-sickness for several years he would not give up but carried out his duties and continued going to sea.

With Kennedy, the mate, in hospital, in 1932 we were three handed. We loaded coal and cement in Barry, part for Plymouth, and the other part for Charlestown in Cornwall. From where we loaded in Barry it was quite a distance to the shops, and thinking we should be in Plymouth on Monday, it being summer time and normally two days sailing to that port, we left with only a very small store of food. For the first twenty four hours we beat to windward down the Channel against a fresh head wind. After passing Lundy, the wind fell to a calm. We motored on but suddenly there was the sound of a crash below, and our engine stopped. The crankshaft was broken and the bottom of the crankcase smashed. The calm lasted for several days, and what little food we had was soon gone. One day we drifted close to a Dutch trawler, fishing some distance away, and I sent my son and the A.B. to ask her captain if he would sell us some fish and bread. The captain asked them what was wrong with our schooner and when he heard that we had only broken down, all the bread he would let them have was a two pound loaf, for which he charged sea price. He then hove up his trawl and steamed in our direction. As he came near, he held up a rope, evidently with visions of salvage. I refused his offer. It was not a tow but a breeze that I wanted. He returned each of the following three days we were becalmed and held up the piece of rope, but I would not look towards him.

A little breeze sprang up, and this took us to Cape Cornwall, where it died out again. I asked several of the fishermen from St. Ives and Sennen who were motoring off to their crab pots, if they could spare us a loaf, but they could not help for they did not carry any food. Later a tug came near, but when she came near enough, it proved to be a tug on the look out for a four-masted barque. They asked me had I seen anything of her, and when I informed them that I had not I asked them would they sell me a loaf.

'No,' they said, 'we came away in a hurry, and each man aboard caters for himself.'

Well, we got into Plymouth at last; our last meal the day before was made from a small packet of pearl barley.

My wife had spent many anxious days waiting for news of our safe arrival, after this slow voyage. After both portions of the cargo had been discharged, we towed round from Charlestown to Par. Our time was up to renew our seaworthiness certificate, and we drydocked in Ben Tregaskes' dock for the survey. Thereafter we were held up in Par for a long time before the engine was in working order again. My wife motored down to Cornwall to spend the whole of this period with me, and apart from the delay and expense to the *Camborne*, we spent a most enjoyable time together.

A very tragic event occurred the following February. We were on passage to Gloucester, and had to anchor off Portishead on account of dense fog, which lasted for several days. The tides were big, and with no wind to blow the fog away I considered it wisest to remain at anchor. I was down below, when my mate, John Kennedy, called to me that a couple of vessels, anchored near us and bound for Gloucester, were getting under way. When I came on deck I could see there was not much of a clearing. It was late afternoon and it would soon be dark, and the River Severn is no place to run any risks with in fog. I said to Kennedy, 'No, Jack, this is no good, it will soon be as bad as ever and the tide runs strong.' He answered, 'Oh, come on Skipper, you know how to navigate the Severn better than they do. Don't let them leave us here.'

The other vessels had left by this time and I was persuaded to start. It is some distance from Portishead to the leading marks and lights that lead the way through the Shoots channel and it is essential to make these marks. Motoring towards the Shoots, I could see no sign whatever of them or in fact of anything. With the fog thickening and settling down, I was about to turn the wheel to return to anchor, when my son suddenly called out in alarm. He called from forward where they had been attempting to cat the anchor, to tell me to pull out the clutch. I immediately did as he said, and my son, as he ran aft, shouted again to me, 'Kennedy is in the water! He has fallen off the anchor!'

The lifebuoys were hung on the sides of the galley. I grabbed one and ran aft. When I got there, Kennedy had just surfaced and I threw the lifebuoy within a foot or two of him. I did not wait to see what he was doing. The *Camborne* was motoring away from him for I had so far had no time to turn the wheel to alter course. Our small boat was towing astern, and the A.B. and my son were pulling at the boat's painter, to haul it close, to go to the rescue. The A.B. slid down the painter and as it seemed too long to wait for my son to slide down with him, I called to the A.B. seaman to let go, and scull the boat as best he could.

All this time, we had been heading towards the Shoots, and as quickly as I could, I put the clutch in and the helm hard over. It seemed an enternity before the schooner made the wide sweep to get her head in the direction where my mate was in the water. It was only then that I had time to see what was happening to him; to my distress I saw that poor Jack was in a panic and was making no effort to reach the lifebuoy. As our boat, being sculled with all possible speed, was nearing him he disappeared. We watched the A.B. pull the boat to the spot where we last saw Jack, and saw him pick up his hat floating on the water.

We returned to anchor. What with the fog, and the stillness, and above all the loss of that fine young life, I spent one of the unhappiest nights of my life.

A short time later, I loaded for Jersey. As a rule, when bound in to St. Helier, I would wait until there was water over the numerous halftide rocks off the harbour. Great care is necessary to go through these channels at low tide, and although I knew the marks for entering, on this occasion I did not use sufficient care. Suddenly, the *Camborne* heeled over, but righted herself and continued on her way, but I was sure she had struck a rock.

We put out the ship's boat. Then we sounded the pump; the hull was not taking in water, but I still wondered if we had escaped damage. After all the years I had been master, it would be most unfortunate if I had damaged my vessel. We docked and discharged in the deep water berth that day. I was impatient to examine my schooner's bottom, so we shifted to the inner dock where she would be dry at low water. When I examined the bottom, my worst fears were realised. About fifty feet of the keel had been sliced off level with the bottom planking, and the planks on the port side were badly scored and bruised. The conditions of my insurance policy were such that I was liable for half the cost of the reconditioning necessary.

Now a fresh difficulty arose. There is no drydock or gridiron in Jersey where we could inspect the exact extent of the damage, and until that was known, neither the underwriters nor the Ministry of Transport would allow me to cross the channel to Par, in Cornwall, where the repairs would be done. My contention was that as the vessel had not taken in water when loaded with a heavy cargo of stone, there could be no risk in sailing empty, but they would not consent until the hull was properly inspected.

At last, after appealing to the Jersey State, I got the loan of some blocks of timber to make a grid, on which the *Camborne* could lie. My crew and I brought these blocks on handcarts to the dock, and the harbour authorities agreed to clamp them down to stop them floating. We put the vessel on the blocks, and the surveyor, after inspecting the damage, advised that he considered it safe for me to proceed to Par for repairs. We arrived there and went into dry dock without further incident and as before my wife came down to stay with me.

Scarfing and fitting a new keel is a very skilful operation but the shipbuilder, Ben Tregaskes, and his men, were well qualified to make a good job of it. At first, we found it difficult to find an elm tree large enough, to saw out the dimensions of timber we required, fifty seven feet by twelve inches by nine inches. Six fine looking trees were sawn through before one was found that was suitable, for most of them had a branch running through the centre of the trunk, with the bark showing red in colour. This the shipbuilder called a 'Rinegall', making the log useless for a keel. Having found the right tree at last, work could commence, but we were eight weeks in dock at Par before we were ready to trade again.

From this time on, one factor on every trip was much the same as the other, that there was very little money to be earned. I mentioned earlier my buying scrap. We had chartered to load salt for Dingle in County Kerry, and I advised the scrap merchants in Briton Ferry of where we were bound, and told them I expected to find a good quantity of scrap there. They agreed to send a representative to arrange the cargo. Some days later, before we sailed, I received an indignant letter from the scrap merchants, to the effect that I should pay the expenses of their representative, for when he had arrived in Ireland to arrange my cargo of scrap, there was not one ton to be bought around Dingle.

When we arrived in that little Irish port, I was approached by a number of young men, who asked me would I be buying scrap. I replied by asking them, had they scrap for sale, and if so, where was it. They said they had none in stock, but if I would buy, they could offer me two hundred tons which they would collect around the countryside. I told them a buyer had been here recently; why had they not sold to him. They did not reply, and I would not give them a decided answer until I had some evidence that there was sufficient scrap to make it worth while buying. We arranged at last that my son Kenneth should hire two bicycles, and he and one of the young men should go together into the countryside and see what quantities of scrap there were. They set off and found a lot, scattered about at farms and blacksmiths. Some of the farmers, when asked had they scrap for sale, replied, 'Scrap for sale, is it? If you are buying scrap, then there is going to be another war.'

The young men were waiting anxiously for my decision to buy, for there was great poverty in the town. All these fine strong young men, with no money and no prospects of earning any. I agreed to buy the scrap at a certain price on delivery at the *Camborne* and to have it weighed on the town scales. The scrap then started to arrive. Where the people got the horses and carts from to haul it with, I do not know. They travelled miles to collect it and within a few days we had taken in over one hundred and sixty tons. The evening before we sailed, I was stopped in the streets, several times, by people I had not met before, who thanked me for being the means of so much money coming into poverty-stricken Dingle.

CHAPTER XVI

The Camborne – our experiences in the terrible gale of February 1936 – back to Tralee – Fenit and a new propeller – Youghal

WHAT A FINE SEABOAT THE *Camborne* WAS. I HAD always thought so, but she proved this in February 1936, when she survived one of the fiercest easterly gales that anyone could remember off the west coast of Britain. We left Gloucester with a cargo of salt for Tralee, and came to anchor the same evening in Cardiff Roads. The following evening we sailed, only to anchor off Angle Bay in Milford Haven. The wind was blowing strong from the south-east. I sent a boat ashore to replenish our stores, and also to send a telegram to my wife, to tell her we had put in for shelter. Several schooners were there, and they had been windbound for some days. Some of their captains came aboard the *Camborne*, and asked me what I thought about making a start. I thought it would be wise to wait another day, though they did not agree with me. They decided to leave, and before long our vessel was the only one left in the anchorage. My son thought we should have sailed with the others, and at last, very much against my better judgement of the weather prospects, we hove up our anchor and got under way.

It was nearly dark when we got to the entrance and I could see one or two of the other schooners putting back to return to anchor. I should have put back with them. Instead, I thought, 'We have a long run ahead, the wind may be strong, but it is fair. I will keep going.'

It was Saturday the 8th of February, and at 11.00 p.m. we were abreast of the Smalls. The wind had by now increased to gale force with mountainous seas. We set a course for the Fastnet, and I stopped the engine and reduced sail. We furled the mizzen and foresail and put two reefs in the mainsail.

By the next day, Sunday the 9th, the wind was even worse, at storm force (force twelve). About 8.00 a.m. a sea broke aboard with such force that it parted the grips holding the ship's boat on the hatch. It was washed about the deck and finally got jammed between the hatch coamings and the rigging. The sea was now breaking aboard the *Camborne* in an alarming manner. It was not safe to run any longer, and so, watching a favourable chance, we pulled the head sails down and brought the schooner into the wind, and lay to under the double reefed mainsail.

The seas were mountainous, the worst I have ever seen. When the vessel was in the hollow of a wave, it would appear that the following sea would engulf her. It was asking a lot of the *Camborne*, fifty two years old, to endure such a battle with the elements. As there was the possibility of a little shelter if we could pass the Fastnet and Cape Clear, I decided we would set the head sails and, this done, I kept the vessel away before the wind and the sea.

At five that afternoon I made a light. It could be either Galley Head or the Fastnet Light, the former being away to the east. The sea was so high it was difficult to discern the character of it. Galley Head had five flashes; the Fastnet, one flash every ten seconds. The distance between the two was twenty-six miles. This was a long way with the amount of sea that was following. It was as well not to look astern. One of my crew belonged to Cape Clear and knew these lights well, and as I could not myself ascertain the one showing, I asked him to go up the rigging and see if he could get the number of flashes. To the relief of all of us, it was the Fastnet.

But we were unable to get any shelter inside Cape Clear and by 6.00 a.m. on Monday the 10th, we were past Mizzen Head and abreast of the Bull Light. The wind was coming off the land in terrific gusts, and at 10.00 a.m. we had been carried past the Skelligs and were off Bray Head. There I was hoping we could have entered Valentia harbour for shelter but the hurricane wind made the attempt quite impossible.

With all the straining and labouring the *Camborne* was making an alarming amount of water. We had three feet of water in the hold. Most of the bulwarks had been washed away, and the seas had broken the engine room skylight, and despite our efforts to effect repair, the water washing about the deck was getting below.

We had all been on deck since Saturday evening without food and without rest, and if our schooner was not to sink, then the water had to be pumped out. I know of no more exhausting work than pumping. It was necessary for the men who were pumping to be secured with ropes, to prevent them being washed overboard, for with the vessel rolling constantly, the force of the water rushing across the deck would wash their feet from under them. Added to all this, there was the bitterly cold wind blowing at gale force from the east. The three young men who were my crew, who had been wet through for days, laboured the whole night through under these conditions. At daybreak on Tuesday the 11th, they reported to me that the pumps had sucked, the water having been pumped out.

By this time, we had been carried many miles away from the land out into the Atlantic. The wind gradually eased, and became a moderate breeze. We were in a dreadful state, most of the sails in ribbons, almost all the bulwarks gone, and the crew completely exhausted. We now had our first real meal since leaving Milford on the Saturday three days before.

I asked my crew to get some spare sails from the sail locker and to bend them, while I went below to see if the engine could be started. Below decks I found everything soaked, the crankcase full of salt water, and I was not able to get it to start. I was still in the engine room at 2.00 p.m. when my son called to me to say a steam trawler was alongside, offering to tow us to safety. I went on deck and thanked him for his offer but although we were in a bad way I did not accept. I felt confident that we could manage without help. The trawler was soon out of sight, and a short time later I had the engine going. Turning the sturdy old *Camborne* due east in the direction where Ireland should be, with the engine running and the sails pulling, we began to make good speed.

We continued to make good progress towards the land and at two o'clock on the morning of Thursday the 13th, I made Loop Head light off the mouth of the Shannon, distant about fifteen miles. The wind was now freshening again with driving snow and visibility was getting poor. Conditions were again getting worse. Just before dawn, about 6.00 a.m. the engine stopped, broken down again. From the bearing I had of Loop Head, by my reckoning we should about fetch Tralee Bay, south of Kerry Head. This was the case and we came to anchor off Samphire Island near Fenit at seven o'clock. It was still blowing hard from the east and bitterly cold.

Before my son or I could think of rest, we had to get our auxiliary in working order. Where we were at anchor off Fenit was too exposed, and we needed power to berth at the pier there. I told the two sailors to turn in, while my son and I endeavoured to find what was wrong with the engine. It was so cold in the engine room and we were so wet and exhausted, that we lit a large brazing blow lamp to give us a little warmth. Eventually we found the fault: the constant flooding of the engine with salt water had seized up the governor. We took it down, cleaned and oiled the parts and then we put it back and had a run out of the engine. By that time it was past midnight. We called the two sailors who had been down below, to take their turn of anchor watch, and we turned into salt water soaked bunks still in our damp clothes and had our first real sleep for six days.

When we were called for breakfast, we went on deck and found the wind had died away and it was calm. There was snow on the mountains south of the Bay and it was still bitterly cold.

Later we were able to get the velocity of the wind from the records kept at Valentia. On the three days from Saturday to Monday it had never blown less than seventy-five miles per hour, and for most of this time in gusts of more than ninety miles an hour. This was the gale when the fine schooner belonging to Youghal, the *Nellie Fleming*, foundered and was lost with all hands, and the Daunt lightship off Cork was blown from her moorings.

After breakfast, we started the engine and hove up the anchor. We had about a mile to sail to Fenit pier. We had been under way but a short time, when the beat of the propeller became so great that the vibration from it shook the vessel. This could mean only one thing, our propeller was a two-bladed one, of cast iron, and evidently one of the blades had broken. This, added to what we had already gone through, was the last straw.

The pilot whose boat I had seen pulling towards us, came on board. I was well known to him and he enquired how we had fared. At that moment, the thump of the propeller and the vibration, was causing me such a worry that I answered. 'I don't know how I am. The engine or something is wrong.'

'Where have you come from?' he asked, 'and how long have you been at sea?'

'Since last Saturday,' I replied.

'Surely not!' he said, 'if you have been at sea since last Saturday then you would not be worrying about a broken propeller!'

I thought our troubles would be over as soon as we moored in the discharging berth. As we came alongside, we were the object of curiosity from quite a large crowd of people on the quay, for we were in a dreadful state, with bulwarks smashed, pieces of tattered and torn sails and frayed ends of ropes, flapping in the wind, the decks washed clean and the ship's boat jammed against the lower rigging. The *Camborne* had come out of the water by the Plimsol mark, where we had pumped away part of the cargo, the salt discharging in the water.

When I went below to stop the engine, I found more serious trouble. In the short time it had been running, the thumping of the one blade of the propeller had shaken loose the packing around the stern tube, and water was rushing in at an alarming rate. I was almost at my wit's end at this. This was a real emergency! I came on deck and called for volunteers from the men on the quay to man the pumps. Several came aboard and started pumping. I phoned the receivers of the cargo to urge them to commence discharge here and not at Tralee but could get no satisfaction from them. The Harbour Master came aboard and demanded to see for himself how fast the water was coming in. When he came on deck, he told me he would get the steam dredger to tow me on to the sand bank, for he said he was not going to see the *Camborne* sink alongside the pier. I begged him not to move so fast and told him we would take a sounding every half hour to see if the pumps were holding their own. I also told him to inform the receivers of the cargo that if they did not take immediate delivery I would jettison it.

We found that by constant pumping the water was not gaining, and because of my ultimatum to the consignees, discharge was started. It was evening by the time half the salt was discharged. The steam dredger then came and towed us to where the water was shallow, and, by this time, I had thought of a plan to stop the inflow of water, by sinking loose bundles of oakum close to the tube. The oakum was sucked into the tube and the leak was stopped.

The pumping cost me £50, quite a lot of money in those days for a day's work. One of my crew went home the day we arrived and I learned later that he never went to sea again. My able seaman went to hospital, and for him this was also his last day at sea. I was surprised when I saw the state of my legs; they were as black as coal and swollen to twice their normal size. What a terrible voyage this had been. I am sure, had the propeller broken when we were off Loop Head, I would not be writing this.

As our cargo, still only half unloaded, was consigned to Tralee, we had to wait for the spring tides before there was sufficient water to proceed there. During this time we packed the stern tube and fitted our spare propeller. When at last we arrived in the dock at Tralee and had finished discharging, it was found that about twenty tons of salt was short, this amount having been pumped out.

Then followed a busy time, for there were repairs to sails, to gear and to the bulwarks. We shipped two fresh sailors, and loaded a cargo of scrap iron and were then under way again.

Our next cargo out was from the Bristol Channel to Youghal. After trading there for so many years, and having so many sailors from Youghal in our vessels, I was well known in the town. The first day I went ashore after arrival, I was stopped by several people who knew we had survived the gale in which the local schooner *Nellie Fleming* was lost. They told me how glad they were to see me safe, and said it was hard to believe any vessel of our size could have survived the terrible seas that had been breaking on Youghal strand during the three days of the storm.

CHAPTER XVII

War again – our Irish trading continues – mines and a fire at sea – the schooner Ryelands *– 1946, my two schooners* Camborne *and* Ryelands *sold – the motor coaster* Eldorita *– I bring my story to an end*

WITH THE THREAT OF WAR IN THE LATE 1930'S, WORK became more plentiful for the coasting trade, and freights began to rise. I was offered a four cylinder Junkers diesel engine of 100 H.P. at a reasonable price, and I bought it, although it was not installed until 1940. My son Kenneth, who had returned from a foreign voyage, sat successfully for his master's certificate. As I was short of a mate, he came to help me on the *Camborne*.

When war broke out again in 1939 to me it seemed like yesterday since the last one ended. Once again began all the difficulties of coastal trading in wartime. Most of the lighthouses were extinguished, others showed only a dim light for a few minutes at intervals and most ports were closed completely after sunset. Patrol boats had to be contacted to obtain the correct signals to pass the signal stations, in order to enter those ports that were open. There were risks of striking drifting mines and of aircraft attack, to say nothing of being bombed after reaching port.

Most of the surviving British schooners were taken over by the Admiralty at this time, to act as anchors outside various harbours for barrage balloons. The thought that my vessel the dear old *Camborne* might be amongst those taken, to be there perhaps for years, was worse to me than the threat of a prison sentence. But we were lucky and our schooner escaped that fate.

We continued on our usual trade, carrying salt from Gloucester to ports on the south and west coasts of Ireland. We had to make our way without escort and it is amazing how we escaped disaster. There were very many risks. An extensive mine field had been laid off the coast of southern Ireland, and after very heavy gales a considerable number of these mines always broke loose from their moorings. At such times, when these mines were washed ashore, explosions would be heard all along the coast. On one voyage on our way back to England, the sea off the Waterford coast was dotted with these drifting mines. We could avoid them in daylight by keeping a good lookout, but after dark we had simply to trust to luck.

At the time of Dunkirk in June 1940, on a passage to Limerick, we had to seek shelter in Valentia. The Customs Officer, who boarded us, was very depressed over our withdrawal from France, and he expressed his sympathy that poor old England was finished at last. He was genuinely sorry. Looking back, it was strange, but it was the furthest thought in my mind that England, in any circumstances, could be finished, and I said so.

On one trip back from Ireland to the Bristol Channel, we received instructions to pass close to the Coningbeg lightship and the Tuskar, before crossing for the Smalls, to clear mine fields. We had a fair wind and the sea was smooth. With our auxiliary working, the new diesel, we made good speed.

When we were abreast of the lightship I saw a distant bright light about four points on the starboard bow. The light increased as we got closer to it and I realised it must be a fire. I thought at first that the oil storage tanks at Milford Haven had been bombed and set ablaze, but as we sailed east and reached the Tuscar and our position to alter course for the Smalls, the fire was now right along our starboard side. There, and as far ahead as I could see, was a blazing inferno with flames roaring towards the sky, from oil and petrol on the surface of the water. It was a most awesome sight. We motored for quite some distance parallel to the fire, and at last, I could see what I considered to be a wide enough gap to motor through. It was a greater risk than I had thought, particularly in a wooden vessel and before the *Camborne* was through, I had a great fear that we would not reach safety. Apparently, we learned later, two large oil tankers had been bombed by German planes and set on fire and it was through the lane separating these two great areas of burning fuel from these ships that we had sailed.

In 1941, my son Humphrey Kenneth became master of the *Irene*[1]. This was the ketch I had sold to Messrs. Colthurst Symons of Bridgwater in 1928. Like me, he traded also to the south of Ireland. But the demand for small coasters to carry cargoes from the steamers discharging at Avonmouth, etc., to the smaller ports in the Bristol

Channel was so great, that we forsook Ireland and took up this trade until the end of the war.

In December of 1942 I bought the schooner *Ryelands*[2] and my son, Humphrey Kenneth, left the *Irene* to take charge of her. For the remaining war years both the *Camborne* and *Ryelands* traded round the Bristol Channel, only going as far south as Penzance or Hayle in Cornwall.

In 1946 we decided to dispose of both the *Camborne* and the *Ryelands* and instead bought the motor coaster *Eldorita*[3]. My son Humphrey took a half share in her and became her master. With the sale of the *Camborne* in that year, I retired. My career at sea was finished after fifty years, forty-two of which I had been master, without any break. These years were one long fight against the elements, the odds against me, working with outdated craft, but it was the life I chose and a life I enjoyed. I wondered what other vocation could have given me so much.

To lose my dear wife only a few years after my retirement was something else in the battle of life I had to accept, and finally, to spend my remaining years after my children were married, alone with my memories. We must accept what comes.

---

[1] The *Irene* continued working until 1960.

[2] The *Ryelands*, built at Glasson Dock and registered at Lancaster in 1887, was a 158-ton 3-masted double topsail schooner. In the 1950's she took a part in films—the first 'Treasure Island' under the name *Hispaniola*. In 1954 she was suitably altered and re-named *Pequod* for a part in the film 'Moby Dick'.

[3] The *Eldorita*, bound for Rotterdam in December 1966, ended her days in the North Sea, thirty-five miles off the Hook of Holland. Having radioed for immediate assistance she reported that she was listing badly, with her engine-room flooded. Her crew were picked up by a German ship.

INDEX

Abersoch, 59 et seq.
Aldridge family, 72, 76, 100, 127
Annalong (Co. Down), 52
Aran Islands, 24
Ardgroom, 128, 129
Arlingham-on-Severn, 72 et seq
Arthurstown (Co. Waterford), 122
Articles of agreement, 28
Auxiliary engines, 93

Bacon cargoes, 116 et seq
Bagillt, 12
Baltimore (Co. Cork), 124, 133
Bardsey Sound, 61
Barrow-in-Furness, 52
Barry, 99, 133
Belfast, 36, 49, 50, 58, 128
Bishop lighthouse, 43
Bridgwater, 76, 100
Bristol, 72, 79, 81
Buncrana, 23, 62

Caernarvon, 57
Caherciveen, 107
Cardiff, 86, 93
Cardigan, 78
Carlingford, 69
Cemlyn Bay (Anglesey), 55
Charles & Eliza Laura (Lifeboat), 126
Charlestown, 133
Cherbourg, 128
Chester, 9, 14
Coasting captains, 10, 11
Coasting life, 25
Collisions, accidents, etc, 63, 87, 89, 136, 146
Connah's Quay, 9 et seq, 22, 29, 32, 35, 41, 44, 47, 49, 57, 74, 76, 128

Cork, 96, 112, 114
Crew of the *Camborne*, 121

Dalbeattie, 70
Dingle, 108, 137
Discharging cargoes, 55, 56, 69
Douglas (I.o.Man), 38, 48
Downpatrick, 44, 45
Dublin, 35, 36, 58
Dungarvan, 98

Ellesmere Port, 63
Engine repairs to the *Camborne*, 117, 129, 142
Erith (Kent), 78
Explosives cargo, 38

Falmouth, 16, 17, 29, 85, 87, 128
Fenit, 103 et seq, 115, 141
Fishers (of Barrow), 95
Flint, 11, 21, 77
Fort William, 29
France, 85, 87 et seq.
Freight rates, 78, 85, 93, 98, 115, 122, 127

Gales, 15, 18, 64, 70, 77, 99, 103, 122, 124, 139 et seq.
Galway, 127
Garston, 59, 69
Gatehouse-of-Fleet, 63
Gloucester, 75, 97, 100, 122, 131, 134, 139
Gravesend, 37
Guernsey, 37

Haverfordwest, 64, 100
Holyhead, 28, 36, 41, 61, 76, 79, 125

Hull, 43
Hyam House (Flint), 40

Innishmore, 23, 24
Irish 'troubles', 93 et seq, 103 et seq.

Jersey, 136

Kelp, 23, 127
Kenmare River, 128, 129
Kennedy, John (seaman), 133, 135
Killorglin, 115
Kilmackilloge, 129
Kinsale, 85
Knight's Town, 104

Lancaster, 69
Land's End, 29, 30
Limerick, 22, 23, 40, 100, 103 et seq.
Liverpool, 18, 47, 58, 116, 118, 131
Liverpool 'flat', 11
Lough Swilly, 26, 62

Manchester, 69
Menai Straits, 46, 57
Mersey, 15, 20, 46, 57
Milford Haven, 43, 64, 100, 139
Minefields, 145
Moelfre Roads, 124
Moorhill (Co. Waterford), 97
Mostyn, 12, 36, 77
Mullaghmore, 23

Newhaven, 41, 121
Newlyn, 34
Newport, 72, 79, 85, 97

Oban, 29

Par, 134, 137
Paulo (dog), 121
Penryn, 78
Pentewan, 16, 17
Penzance, 64, 147
Perth, 122
Pilots, 42, 60, 71, 88
Plymouth, 82, 133
Point of Ayr colliery, 11, 62
Portishead, 134, 135
Portmadoc, 59, 93, 95
Preston, 41, 42, 71

Queensborough, 27, 29
Queenstown, 117

Ramsey (I.o.Man), 62
River Dee, 9
Rochester, 29
Rosslare, 59
Runcorn, 18, 64
Rutland in the Rosses, 23

Sailing without ballast, 131
Saltash, 43
Saltmey, 14
Scrap-iron cargoes, 131, 137
Severn Bore, 75
Shannon, 23, 103, 108, 141
Shaw, Captain Hugh: childhood 9 et seq; as a cook 22 et seq; in court 31; as A.B 36 et seq; as mate 40; as captain 44; loses anchor, 52, 53; becomes owner 57; his future wife 73; encounter with U. boat 91; sons of, 128, 145, 146; scrap-iron buying 131; retirement 147
Shaw, Captain Humphrey, 11, 39, 122

150 INDEX

Shaw, Captain William, 100
Swansea, 15, 16, 40, 90

Tarbet, 113, 114
Torpedoing, 91
Tralee, 108, 111, 115 et seq, 139, 143, 144
Tugs, 13, 14

U-Boats, 82, 86, 91
Ulverston, 15
Uncle Tom (mate), 45, 46
Unusual cargoes, 108, 128

Valentia Island, 103, 117, 140, 146
Vessels lost at sea, 59, 60, 78, 125, 142
Vessels, sailing:
  Alfred, 15, 18
  Camborne, 100 et seq, 139
  Despatch, 75
  Earl Cairns, 75
  Earl of Latham, 17, 20
  Elizabeth Drew, 75
  Elizabeth Hyam, 39 et seq, 44, 49, 51
  Emma and Esther, 33 et seq
  Enterprise, 18
  Excel, 124 et seq
  Harvest Queen, 78
  Hilda, 39
  Irene, 100, 108, 116, 127
  Isabella, 42, 45

  J.C.R., 57 et seq
  Kate, 76 et seq, 90, 116
  Kindly Light, 84, 86
  Lady Fielding, 59, 60
  Lizzie, 36, 37
  Mary Elisabeth, 22 et seq
  M. E. Johnson, 64
  Mary Miller, 95
  Nellie Fleming, 142
  Not Forgot, 35
  Ryelands, 147
  Sarah Latham, 58, 61
  Sunbeam, 39
  Victor, 40

Vessels, steam and motor:
  Albert, 14, 41
  Alice Capper, 14
  Coronia, 110
  Eldorita, 147
  Great Eastern, 15
  Lucerne, 63
  Manxman, 14
  Nordstad, 128
  Taliesin, 14

Waterford, 43, 59, 123
Wildroads, 11, 22, 35, 48, 77
World War I, 79 et seq
World War II, 145

Youghal, 79 et seq, 99, 107, 144

The WRECK AND RESCUE Series (*General Editor: Grahame Farr*) are standard histories of Britain's lifeboats, recording the story of each station from its inception to the present day, complete with Boat and Service Records. They also detail innumerable stories of shipwrecks round this island's shores, and include many historic photographs.

WRECK AND RESCUE ROUND THE CORNISH COAST
Cyril Noall and Grahame Farr

I. THE STORY OF THE NORTH COAST LIFEBOATS
Bude — Port Isaac — Padstow — Newquay — Hayle
126 *pages* . 14 *plates* . *maps*

II. THE STORY OF THE LAND'S END LIFEBOATS
St. Ives — Sennen — Isles of Scilly — Penzance — Newlyn — Penlee — Porthleven
151 *pages* . 29 *plates* . *maps*

III. THE STORY OF THE SOUTH COAST LIFEBOATS
Mullion — The Lizard — Cadgwith — Coverack — Porthoustock — Falmouth — Portloe — Mevagissey — Polkerris — Fowey — Looe
195 *pages* . 29 *plates* . *maps*

WRECK AND RESCUE IN THE BRISTOL CHANNEL
Grahame Farr

I. THE STORY OF THE ENGLISH LIFEBOATS
Clovelly — Appledore — Northam Burrows — Braunton Burrows — Morte Bay — Ilfracombe — Lynmouth — Minehead — Watchet — Burnham — Weston-super-Mare
183 *pages* . 26 *plates* . *maps*

II. THE STORY OF THE WELSH LIFEBOATS
Penarth — Barry Dock — Atlantic College — Porthcawl — Port Talbot — Swansea — The Mumbles — Port Eynon — Llanelli — Burry Port — Pembrey — Ferryside — Tenby — Angle
190 *pages* . 28 *plates* . *maps*

WRECK AND RESCUE ON THE ESSEX COAST
Robert Malster

> THE STORY OF THE ESSEX LIFEBOATS
> Harwich — Walton — Frinton — Clacton — Southend-on-Sea — the salvaging smacks — the lifeboat builders of Essex
> 168 *pages*   .   30 *plates*   .   *maps*

WRECK AND RESCUE ON THE COAST OF DEVON
Grahame Farr

> THE STORY OF THE SOUTH DEVON LIFEBOATS
> Plymouth — Yealm River — Hope Cove — Salcombe — Dartmouth — Brixham/Torbay — Torquay — Teignmouth — Exmouth — Sidmouth
> 196 *pages*   .   37 *plates*   .   *maps*

WRECK AND RESCUE ON THE COAST OF WALES
Henry Parry

> I. THE LIFEBOATS OF CARDIGAN BAY AND ANGLESEY
> Barmouth — Criccieth/Portmadoc — Pwllheli — Abersoch — Porthdinllaen — Llanaelhaiarn — Llanddwyn — Rhosneigr — Rhoscolyn — Holyhead
> 148 *pages*   .   20 *plates*   .   *maps*

> II. THE STORY OF THE NORTH WALES LIFEBOATS
> Cemlyn — Cemaes — Bull Bay — Moelfre — Penmon — Beaumaris — Llandudno — Llandulas — Abergele — Rhyl — Point of Ayr — Mostyn

WRECK AND RESCUE ON THE DORSET COAST
Grahame Farr

> THE STORY OF THE DORSET LIFEBOATS
> Lyme Regis — Portland — Weymouth — Kimmeridge — Chapman's Pool — Swanage — Studland — Poole
> 135 *pages*   .   29 *plates*   .   *maps*

D. BRADFORD BARTON LTD
TRETHELLAN HOUSE   .   TRURO   .   CORNWALL